PEN ART

in

Snap! Programming

*the art of programming and
the programming of art*

1st edition

Abhay B. Joshi • **Sandesh R. Gaikwad**

Book series on "Learning computer programming and CS principles"

To Brian Harvey,
Whose Logo interpreter helped us become turtle programmers long before Scratch and
Snap were created

Published by:
SPARK Institute and Publications
3554 - 173rd CT NE
Redmond, WA 98052, USA
1st edition: 11 April 2019

Cover design by:
Ravindra Pande

To order your digital copy:
Go to Amazon.com

To order your printed copy:
Go to Amazon.com or write to: abjoshi@yahoo.com
Check pricing at: http://www.abhayjoshi.net/spark/snap/psnap.pdf

Other books in this series:
Learn CS Concepts with Snap
Advanced Scratch Programming

Click http://www.abhayjoshi.net/spark/csseries.pdf to see the complete list.

Foreword

We now accept the fact that learning is a lifelong process of keeping abreast of change. And the most pressing task is to teach people how to learn. - Peter Drucker

Background

This book is another in the series of programming books written by the authors who believe in the idea of using *computer programming as a medium for learning* (or *"constructionism"*, using the jargon of experts). The benefits of learning programming and *computer science* concepts well before college are now well-understood.

Here is a list of some of the amazing things that happen when young students engage in computer programming:

- They become *active* and *creative* learners, because they explore ideas through a hands-on activity with an infinitely powerful tool.
- They learn to think about and analyze *their own thinking*, because that is the only way to program computers.
- They learn to solve complex problems by breaking them into smaller sub-problems.
- They learn a new way of problem-solving (called "computational thinking").
- In the world of programming, answers are not simply "right" or "wrong"; this prepares one's mindset for real-life problems.
- Their learning processes are transformed from *acquiring facts* to *thinking creatively and analytically*.

About this book

In this book, we are going to focus on the "Pen" feature of the popular Snap! programming language. Henceforth we will refer to "Snap!" simply as "Snap".

It is assumed that the reader is familiar with the basic features of Snap, such as, motion commands and looping. There is a lot of material on Snap Programming on the Internet, including videos, online courses, Snap projects, and so on. We highly recommend the book "**Learn CS Concepts with Snap**" by one of the authors, if you are a complete newcomer to Snap, or if you wish to brush up on your concepts.

However, as you will discover, you can become an accomplished "Pen Artist" (or "Turtle Programmer") without having to be an expert Snap programmer. We have explained relevant Snap commands and concepts wherever required.

Audience

This book is expected to allow anyone to experience the magic of Turtle programming. You can read and understand the concepts presented, try out sample programs, and exercise your creativity by trying out the exercises. There are plenty of examples presented along with their results.

The book is meant for CS students of all ages, teachers, parents, and really anyone who wants to get the wonderful taste of the entertaining and creative aspect of Computer Programming.

How the book is organized

The book is organized as a series of chapters – each containing a bunch of concepts and associated programming activities. Every chapter includes review questions and several programming assignments that will help you practice all the concepts learnt till then. Answers to all "review questions" and links to working programs for most of the programming exercises in the book are available online. Download them at:

http://abhayjoshi.net/spark/snap/book2/solutions.pdf.

Hardware and Software

You can do all your Snap programming work online by creating your own account at http://snap.berkeley.edu.

Acknowledgements

We wish to thank Ravindra Pande for creating a truly beautiful cover for the book.

We wish to thank TEALS (https://www.tealsk12.org) – a nonprofit organization dedicated to the cause of teaching computer science to all high school students – for allowing the authors to teach Snap using their remote classroom infrastructure.

Finally, this book would not have been possible without the constant encouragement of our friends and family.

We do hope that you will find this book useful and enjoyable.

Abhay B. Joshi
abjoshi@yahoo.com

Seattle, USA
11 April 2019

Sandesh R. Gaikwad
sandyg31794@gmail.com

Pune, India
11 April 2019

Authors' background

As a freelance teacher, Abhay's area of interest is teaching Computer Programming as "the exciting new magic" and also as "a medium for learning" in the constructivist tradition. He has been teaching regularly to elementary, middle, and high school students in WA, USA and Pune, India since 2008. He teaches at Aksharnandan School in Pune, India every summer, and works with TEALS (http://tealsk12.org/) to teach Computer Science to high school students in the US. Since 2011, he has authored or co-authored several programming books, which are based on Scratch, Snap, and Logo. Abhay has been associated with the Software Industry since 1988 as a programmer, product developer, entrepreneur, and teacher. After getting an MS in Computer Engineering from Syracuse University (USA), he worked as a software engineer for product companies that developed operating systems, network protocols, and secure software. In 1997, Abhay co-founded Disha Technologies, which grew to become a successful software services organization.

As a Project Management and ERP consultant, Sandesh is actively involved in the training, coaching and mentoring of software professionals on technical topics as well as on leadership, communication, and project management. Sandesh started his career in the software industry in 1991 and has worked across the globe in a variety of roles. Prior to that he was a lecturer and taught assembly language and Pascal programming to engineering students. He has been teaching computer programming to high school students since 2008.

Programming remains a favorite hobby of the authors, and they continue to explore the "entertaining, intellectual, and educational" aspects of programming.

Abhay lives in Seattle, USA and Sandesh lives in Pune, India.

Contents

Chapter 1:
Getting Started with Snap Turtle

A drawing is simply a line going for a walk. — Paul Klee

What we will learn in this chapter

- Snap Turtle: a special triangle-shaped costume
- Pen commands
- Motion commands to actually draw on the screen
- Concepts of movement (distance) and direction (angle).
- How to draw simple shapes

Introduction

Take a look at the following design. It appears like a beautiful night sky filled with hundreds of colorful stars.

Figure 1.1

A powerful feature of Snap called "Pen art" allows you to draw this and many such beautiful graphical designs.

In this book, we are going to focus on this "Pen" feature of the popular Snap programming language. Some basic knowledge of Snap is assumed, but, as you will discover, you can become an accomplished "Pen Artist" (or "Turtle Programmer") without having to be an expert Snap programmer. We have explained relevant Snap commands and concepts wherever required.

Pen Art aka Turtle Programming

Snap (and Scratch, from which Snap was derived) borrowed the pen feature from another older language called "Logo". And Logo contained a single sprite – a triangular shape called "Turtle"! This Turtle had a pen attached to it. And so, as it followed instructions and was moved around on the screen, it drew lines. Hence, the entire field of drawing shapes in Logo came to be called "Turtle Programming". There is even a field of geometry called "Turtle Geometry". Modern languages, such as Python, have the aptly-named "Turtle" libraries that implement the drawing feature of Logo.

Snap, being a descendant of Logo, includes the Pen. Every sprite in Snap has a pen attached to it (just like the Turtle did in Logo). When the pen is put down (using the "pen down" command), the sprite starts drawing on the screen as it moves around.

Since our focus in this book is entirely on "Pen Art" we have no use for the hundreds of costumes provided by the Snap library. We will use the original triangle-shaped costume called "Turtle" in all our Snap programs in this book.

But, of course, you may use any costume you like, since the pen remains attached to the belly of every sprite no matter which costume it wears!

So, remember, now on when we say "Turtle", we are simply referring to the Pen attached to any sprite.

Drawing with the Snap Turtle

Can we get the Snap Turtle to draw things on the screen, like those shown below?

Figure 1.2

The answer is Yes! We can create these and many other exciting drawings with the help of the Snap Turtle! Let us get introduced to this new friend.

As mentioned already, every sprite in Snap has a pen attached to it (at its center) and is able to draw on the background. The pen commands are listed under the "Pen" category and they contain commands to put the pen down (after which the sprite will start drawing whenever it moves), pen up (after which the drawing will stop), set pen size, set pen color (renamed as "set pen hue" in Snap 5), and so on.

clear command clears all drawing created by all sprites.

pen down and **pen up** commands start and stop leaving a pen trail respectively.

`set pen size to ◯` and `change pen size by ◯` determine the thickness of the pen. There is no upper limit on pen size. The shape of the tip of the pen, i.e., that of a dot drawn by it, is exactly circular.

The actual drawing happens when the sprite moves using motion commands. Using cleverly designed scripts, you can draw practically any type of geometric patterns. For example, the following script draws a square:

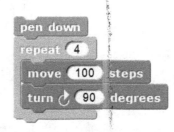

Programming practice

1. Using the Snap pen and motion commands draw the following shapes.

Using Colors

In an earlier demo program, we saw many colors. How do we get the Turtle to draw colorful lines?

Easy! Snap uses the following commands to make your drawings colorful:

`set pen color to ■` sets the pen color to the color shown. By clicking first on the color square and then anywhere on the Snap window, you may choose a color of your liking.

`set pen color to ●` and `change pen color by ●` also control the pen color by using integers to represent colors. There are 200 colors in Snap numbered 1 to 200.

In addition, you can control shade by using the commands `set pen shade to ●` and `change pen shade by ●`.

Thus, the real color on the screen is a result of color and shade.

The following commands will draw a colorful "Hi".

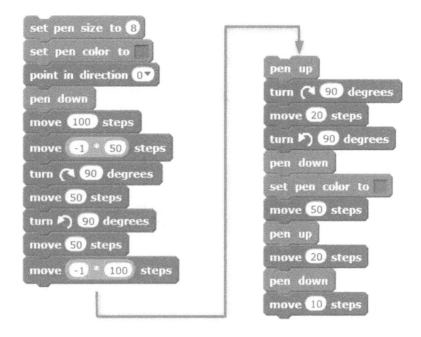

Turtle State

As you might have observed, the Turtle has certain properties, such as, its position on the screen and its orientation. The collection of all such properties is called its "state". Can you think of what else would be part of the "Turtle state"?

Here is the complete list:
1. Screen position (where on screen it is)
2. Orientation (which way it is facing)
3. Pen position (up or down)
4. Pen color
5. Pen thickness

As programmers, we must be aware of the Turtle state throughout our program, since it has impact on how the Turtle will behave. For example, if the pen is up, our motion commands are not going to draw anything.

Programming practice

2. Draw the shapes shown in the collage Figure 1.2.

3. Can you write Snap instructions to draw the shape shown here?

Insights and tips

- If you need blank space, you must use the "pen up" and "pen down" commands.
- "Set pen color" does not change the color of what is already drawn. It's like dipping your brush in a new color.
- Common problems:
  - Sometimes we forget to give the "pen down" command after a "pen up" command, and then wonder why nothing is getting drawn on the screen.
  - Sometimes the Turtle will draw in unexpected directions. That's because we have lost track of the direction the Turtle is facing.
- The Turtle can draw even when it's invisible. But, keep it visible while it is drawing things for you, so that you know its current position and direction.

Chapter 1: Getting Started with Snap Turtle

Chapter 2:
Designs with Repeating Patterns

Computers are good at following instructions, but not at reading your mind.
— Donald Knuth

What we will learn in this chapter
- Using REPEAT to draw designs that contain repeating patterns.
- REPEAT is a labor-saving idea – not for the computer, but for us.
- REPEAT is also a powerful idea – something that opens up new possibilities.

Introduction
Take a look at the following design. It appears like a powerful multi-color star.

Figure 2.1

Do we know enough of Turtle programming to draw this star? Probably not. There is actually a powerful new way to draw this star (and many other exciting designs) quite easily. Read on to learn about it.

Designs with repetition

Before we tackle the star, let us consider a simpler design:

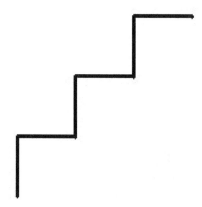

We can easily draw it using Snap blocks from the "Motion" and "Pen" pallets.

Do you see a repeating pattern in the picture? Do you see that a single *stair* is drawn 3 times? A single stair can be drawn using:

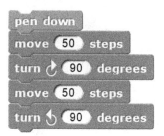

Of course, the Turtle should be pointing in the correct direction (North) before running this script. And then, if we run the same sequence 3 times, we will get the above staircase.

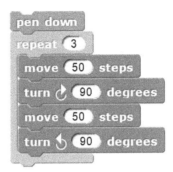

How about drawing a dashed line?

How about drawing a rectangle wave?

Do you see a repeating pattern in each of these?

Just like the staircase, there is a basic pattern (that is repeated) in each of the above pictures. If we can work out the script for each basic pattern, we can simply use this script a number of times to get the final picture.

So, for each of these pictures a certain script needs to be *repeated*.

In each of these cases, we can simply use the REPEAT command in the "control" category to perform the repetition for us.

Let's take another look at this command block.

How to use the REPEAT command

Let's try this procedure to say "I am an idiot" 4 times!

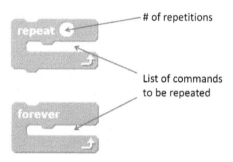

The basic format of these procedures is as follows:

# of repetitions

List of commands
to be repeated

Dashed line

Let's look at the dashed line in the figure above once more.

If you look carefully, you will notice that the basic pattern is this: a visible dash followed by an invisible dash. The following script would draw this basic pattern.

To draw this basic pattern 5 times, we use the REPEAT procedure:

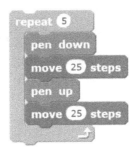

Programming practice

1. For each of the shapes shown below:
    - Figure out the basic pattern that is repeated. Also note the starting position and orientation of the Turtle.
    - Develop a script for the basic pattern and run it multiple times to see if it works as expected.
    - Develop a script (using the repeat block) to draw the shape.

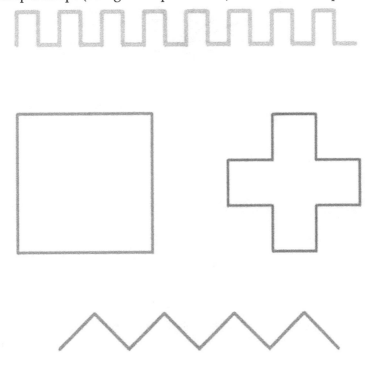

Drawing a star using REPEAT

Ok, you think that REPEAT saves script editing effort. And you are right. But, REPEAT is much more interesting than just being an "editing assistant". Drawing a star (as below) gives us a perfect opportunity to glimpse the power of REPEAT.

Let's say we want to draw the "point star" as shown here.

It is basically a bunch of rays (line segments) coming out of a point. Right? This star has 20 rays. And the gap (angle) between each adjacent pair of rays is constant.

Let's see how we would go about drawing such a star using blocks from the "Motion" and "Pen" pallets.

To simplify the problem, let us first try a star with fewer rays.

This star below has 6 rays. We will assume that the Turtle is initially at the center. After drawing each ray (moving forward and back), the Turtle has to take a right turn. Since there are 6 equal turns, each of these turns (angles) must be 60 (360/6).

The following partial attempt to draw the above star shows how a repeating pattern is emerging:

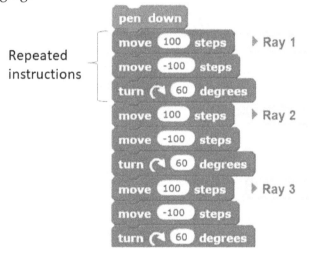

Clearly, REPEAT would help here:

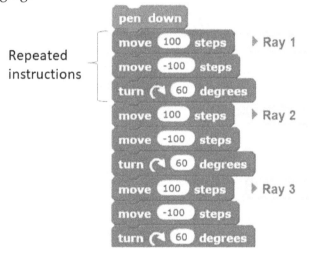

Point star with 20 rays

Now, can you draw the star shown earlier which consists of 20 rays? If you use a similar logic, you would come up with the following:

- the number of rays is 20
- the number of turns would be 20
- so, each turn would be 360/20 = 18

Type the following instruction and see what happens!

```
pen down
repeat 20
    move 100 steps
    move -100 steps
    turn 18 degrees
```

Actually, we can decide to be lazy and write the script to even perform the calculations for us:

```
pen down
repeat 20
    move 100 steps
    move -100 steps
    turn 360 / 20 degrees
```

Programming practice

2. Do you feel you can draw a star of any size and any number of rays? Try the following:

    a. Red star with 20 rays of length 100
    b. Green star with 40 rays of length 200
    c. Orange star of 10 rays of length 50

3. Can you now write a script to draw the colorful star shown in Figure 2-1? (Hint: Consider drawing 3 stars on top of each other.)

4. How about converting the star into this next earth-like picture?

Review Questions

1. State if the following statement is True or False.
   The script contained inside the REPEAT block should include instructions to set the initial position and orientation for the Turtle.

2. We want to draw four vertical lines parallel to each other as shown below. The following script gives us the figure on the right. Can you figure out the error and correct the script?

```
pen down
repeat 4
    move 100 steps
    move -100 steps
    turn ↻ 90 degrees
    move 60 steps
    turn ↺ 90 degrees
```

3. The following script is expected to draw the figure shown next to it. Identify the missing instruction. (Assumption: The Turtle is facing north, i.e. pointing up, initially).

Insights and tips

- The REPEAT block saves us the labor of repetitive tasks, although the computer does the same amount of work.
- Before using REPEAT, you must first figure out (in your mind or notebook) what exactly is getting repeated in your design. The repeating pattern usually has two components: (a) visible and (b) invisible (usually turns or jumps).
- To confirm our understanding, we should write the script for the basic pattern and run it a number of times.
- The best way to figure out the repeating pattern:
  - o Assume a starting position.
  - o Imitate the Turtle movement yourself or using some object (preferably something that clearly shows the orientation).
  - o Include all the steps till you come back to your initial orientation (the position may be different).
- The following should NOT be included inside the REPEAT block:
  - o Instructions to set the initial position and orientation of the Turtle.
  - o Instructions to set the initial pen properties (up/down, size, color, etc.).

Chapter 3:
Teaching New Words

Some of the best programming is done on paper, really. Putting it into the computer is just a minor detail. — Max Kanat-Alexander

What we will learn in this chapter
- How to create new custom blocks.
- What is "Abstraction".
- How to edit (modify, rename or delete) custom blocks.
- How to make custom blocks flexible and powerful by giving them input.

Introduction

So far, we have been creating interesting shapes and designs using standard command blocks available in Snap. Wouldn't it be fun if we could create our own Snap commands?

For example, it would be nice if we had our own custom block called **Blocks** to draw the structure shown below.

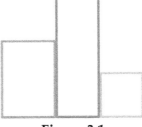

Figure 3.1

The good news is we can indeed create such custom blocks. In this chapter, we will learn how to create custom blocks and use them in powerful ways.

Procedures, blocks and instructions – quick review

A *procedure* is like a recipe of how to do something. Most of the Snap blocks are *procedures*. For example, the move block is a procedure that knows how to move a sprite. Snap blocks are thus individual procedures that carry out specific tasks.

A Snap *instruction* consists of a combination of one or more blocks that we drag and drop in the script area, and which is then run by Snap when we click on it. For example, the following instruction evaluates the expression 20*30 and shows 600 on the screen.

A Snap instruction, like the one above, always carries out a specific, well-defined, and repeatable task. If you look carefully, you will notice that the instruction above contains the say block ![say for secs] and the multiplication block ![multiply] . In other words, every Snap instruction consists of one or more blocks.

New Snap blocks

At the bottom of every pallet, is a button labeled "Make a block." You can also right-click in the script area and then choose "Make a block" from the menu. A dialog appears in which you can specify the name and type of the procedure. "Command" is a procedure without a return value and "Reporter" is a procedure that has a return value (and is also known as a "function"). "Predicate" is a reporter procedure that reports Boolean (true or false) values. We will not use the "predicate" type in this book.

The following picture shows that we are creating a new "command" procedure called "Greeting".

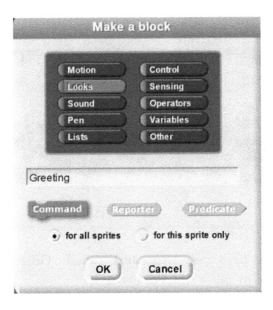

We have selected the "Looks" category (palette) for this new block.

When you click Ok, you see this dialog box:

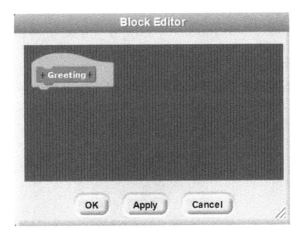

Below the hat block "Greeting" you create a script by attaching existing Snap command blocks. This is what I created:

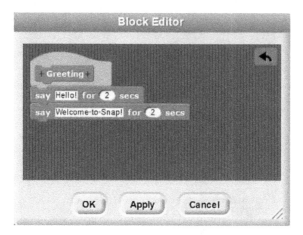

Clicking "OK" gives us a new procedure called "Greeting" in the "Looks" palette. You can use it in any script. For example:

Right-click on this new block and select "edit" if you wish to further modify it.

Review questions

1. The following script shows the definition of a new procedure called "Jump". How can I use this new procedure in my Snap program?

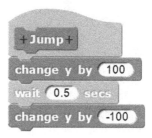

   A. By clicking anywhere on this definition
   B. By sending a broadcast "jump"

C. By using the new block  in my script

D. By saving this definition in a separate project

Programming practice

1. Create a custom block `Staircase` that will draw a staircase of 4 steps. Refer to the instructions below which draw a 3-step staircase.

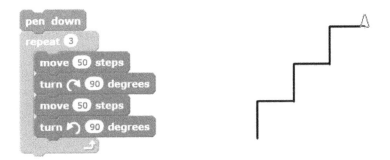

2. Create a new block "`Letter T`" that draws the letter T.

3. Create a custom block "`Blocks`" that draws the shape in Figure 3.1.

4. Create a custom block "`PointStar`" that draws a star with 20 rays each 100 steps long (we learnt how to draw a point star in a previous chapter).

5. Define a new custom block "`Letter Z`" that draws the letter Z as shown below. Then, modify the same custom block to add curls as shown in the next picture.

Best practices

Before you create new custom blocks, if you take care of the following, you will spend less time debugging problems in your new blocks!

- As far as possible, avoid using names same as or similar to standard Snap blocks.
- Use names that describe their purpose.
- Use comments to record assumptions about the initial state of the sprite.
- Try out pieces of script before putting them in the block definition.
- Test the new custom block under different conditions.
- While defining a custom block that draws something on the stage, put `pen down` at the beginning and `pen up` at the end.

Abstraction

Abstraction is an interesting concept which means capturing an idea into a single word (or phrase), image, map, audio clip, etc. In our day-to-day life we assign words to complex concepts or ideas. For example, "pedestrian" is an abstraction for *a person walking on a footpath*. Once we assign such words to ideas, we can refer to the ideas simply through those words.

Similarly, our new Snap procedure "Jump" is the abstraction for the idea of moving a sprite some distance up and down. Defining a new word that has a specific meaning is called abstraction.

Programming practice

Define the following new custom blocks. Verify that these new blocks work as expected.

6. For geometric shapes like rectangle and triangle.

7. For English letters (stick or block) like i, H, E, or A.

8. For a rectangle wave.

9. To draw the following design:

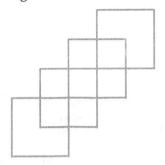

New blocks and old blocks

Once defined, a new custom block is treated by Snap just like any other block that Snap already knows. There is no special treatment for new custom blocks. For example, if you want to define yet another new block, you can make use of both the standard blocks provided with Snap and the new custom blocks that you have created.

Let's say we want to draw a chain of the letter X, i.e. three of them side by side. We will first create a new custom block called **LetterX** to draw X. We will then use the following steps to draw a chain of 3 X's:

Repeat 3 times:
1. Draw X.
2. Position the Turtle at the right upper corner of X.

We can create a new custom block **chain** for this entire procedure as shown below.

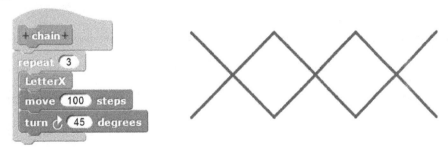

Custom blocks with inputs

With the ideas we have learnt so far – use of Snap blocks to create Scripts, creating new custom blocks, and the REPEAT command block – can we draw some of the designs shown below?

Figure 3.2

We probably can. For instance, we can use the 'PointStar' custom block, which we created earlier in one of the programming exercises. But, we will have to constantly modify the procedure to draw the variety shown above. Snap offers an idea that allows a single PointStar procedure to draw all of the stars above. Won't that be interesting? So, read on to learn this new idea.

Creating custom blocks that take input:

The behavior of many Snap blocks depends on how they are invoked. It depends on the *input* supplied. For instance, **move ⬤ steps** can do its job only when you tell it *how many* steps to move. Or, **wait ⬤ secs** block needs to know *how many* seconds to wait. So, when we say 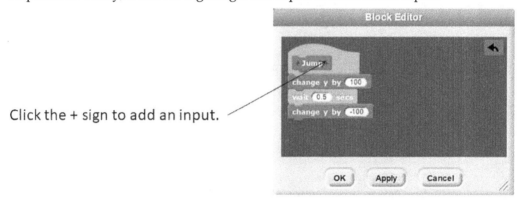, "10" is the input to the move block. Similarly, includes an input of "1" to the wait block.

Snap allows you to define new custom procedures which take input. Right-click the new block "Jump" (which we defined earlier) and click "edit". You will see the block editor again.

We will add to "Jump" a *number* input labeled as "height". The label has no importance really, other than giving a descriptive name to the input.

Click the + sign to add an input.

You will see this input editor:

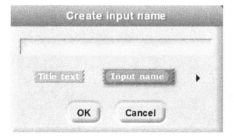

Type the name "height". Click the small arrow to choose your input type. In our case, the type is *number*. After clicking OK, you will see the following:

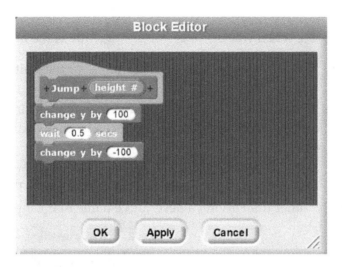

Now, the input is useful only if it is actually used in the procedure. You can drag the new input and drop it wherever appropriate in your sequence of commands. This is how our final "Jump" procedure will look:

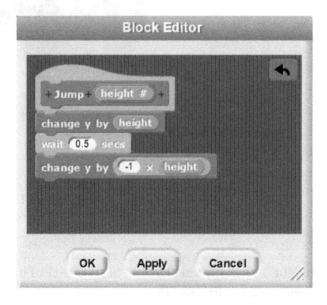

Note that we have to use the "multiply" operator in the second "change y" command to make the change negative.

If I use this new procedure in a script, say, as 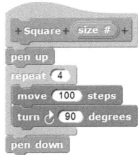, the sprite will jump up and down by 100 steps.

Review questions

2. Every Snap block requires input. True or False?

3. You can change the value of the input inside the custom block. True or False?

4. A sprite has a new block called "Square" as shown below. Which of the following is true?

a. It will draw a square as big as the input "size".
b. It will not draw anything.
c. It will draw a square of size 100.
d. It will not draw a square but a set of 4 connected lines.

5. The following script uses the "Jump" custom block defined earlier. How will the sprite behave when we run this script?

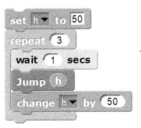

a. It will not jump at all.

b. It will jump 50 steps only once.

c. It will jump 3 times: 50 steps each time.

d. It will jump 3 times: 50, 100 and 150 steps respectively.

Programming practice

10. Create a custom block to draw hexagons of any size.

11. Create a custom block "Dashed Line" that draws a dashed line. The input specifies number of dashes.

Using multiple inputs

Our custom blocks can have as many inputs as we want. For example, we can create a custom block that takes 3 numbers and adds them together:

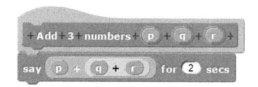

Enter whatever input you want, click on the custom block and confirm that you get the right answer. Add 3 numbers 2 3 4 will give 9.

Or, consider the waveform custom block that draws a rectangle waveform:

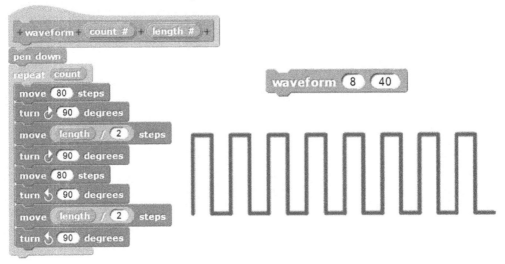

This always draws 5 wavelets. We will add one input (called *count*) to control the *number* of wavelets. We will use it in the repeat block in place of 5 (since the number 5 determines the number of wavelets).

Next, we will add a second input (called *length*) to control the *wavelength* of the wavelets. We will need to use it in the move block in place of 40 (since '40' determines half of the wavelength of each wavelet).

Review questions

6. When we edit a custom block definition and change the name of its input, Snap automatically changes the script to reflect the new name of the input wherever it is used. True or False?

Programming practice

12. Add a 3rd input to **waveform** ◯ ◯ above to control the height of each wavelet.
13. Create custom blocks with 2 inputs for: (a) Staircase, (b) PointStar.
14. Create a custom block that draws a night sky of many point stars (of different sizes and colors).
15. Create a custom block that draws a collage of different shapes (of different sizes and colors) on the screen as shown in Figure 3.2.

Procedures with return values:

What do we mean by "returning" a value? Let's consider a couple of examples. The Snap blocks "pick random" or "join" (both in the Operators pallet) not only perform some well-defined function, but also *return* something. For instance, "pick random" *returns* a number, "join" *returns* a string. In CS lingo, such procedures that *return* a value are called "Functions". In Snap, they are called "reporters". Snap provides the block **report** ▢ to allow a procedure to return a value.

So far we have only created procedures that do something but don't return anything. They are similar to Snap blocks such as "move" and "turn" which similarly do not return anything.

Let us now learn how to create our own *reporters*. Let us say we want to create a reporter "max" that takes two numbers as input and returns the bigger one of the two.

The following picture shows how to create a reporter procedure "max":

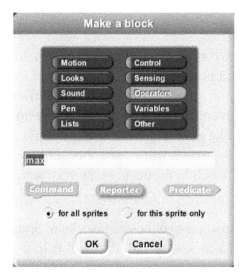

The following script shows the definition of this new block called "max".

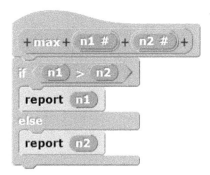

As you can see, it takes n1 and n2 as input and returns the bigger of the two.

Try running the following commands to verify that "max" works correctly:

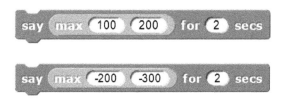

Insights and tips

- Input allows us to control the behavior of our custom blocks. They become highly flexible and powerful.
- Before using input, make a custom block without input, make sure it works, and then identify where you want to use input.
- If you want to make a custom block with multiple inputs, add one input at a time; test to make sure it works, and then add the next one.
- Add meaningful labels to inputs to make your script readable.

Final "word"

The pun is intended. Creating new custom blocks in Snap is not just fun, but, as you will discover later, a necessary skill that will help you build interesting and complex programs. Custom blocks are an essential element of a powerful problem-solving idea called "decomposition" or "divide and conquer". So, create new custom blocks whenever possible.

Chapter 4:
Drawing Polygons and Circles

Programming isn't about what you know; it's about what you can figure out.
— Chris Pine

What we will learn in this chapter
- Turtle Round Trip (TRT) principle.
- Drawing regular polygons, circles, and stars using the TRT principle.
- Scaling objects by increasing their size without changing their shape.

Introduction
The time has come for us to teach the Turtle a bit of Geometry! When we speak of Geometry the things that come to our mind are lines, triangles, squares, hexagons, circles, etc. See below a few designs drawn using these shapes.

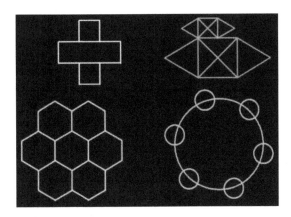

In this chapter, we will see how we can teach Snap to draw this sort of shapes called regular polygons - meaning polygons having all sides of equal length.

Turtle round trips

Round trip is a trip that brings the Turtle back to its original state (screen position as well as orientation). There is something special about round trips. We will try to discover it through a couple of experiments.

Let's begin with a simple round trip along a rectangle. We know that the following script will draw a 100 x 200 rectangle and bring the Turtle back to its original state:

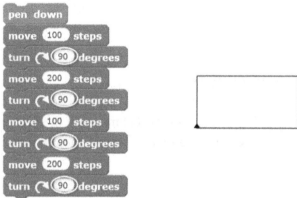

Run these instructions to ensure it is a true round trip. Now, add up all the turns the Turtle has taken in this round trip. You will notice that *the total comes to 360.*

Now, let's try a slightly complicated round trip as shown below:

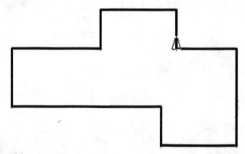

Write a script to perform this round trip, and once again, add up all the turns the Turtle has taken in this round trip. **Important**: Count right turns as *positive* and left turns as *negative. You will discover that the sum is 360.* (We ignore the sign of the total.)

Programming practice

1. Take the Turtle on a round trip that looks like a closed T shape and measure the total turns taken by the Turtle.

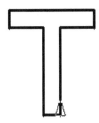

2. Take the Turtle through a couple of free round trip travels around the screen, such that the Turtle roams around the screen, takes turns, and returns home with the original heading. Each time add up the angles. Just remember that a left turn should be counted as negative, and right turn as positive.

Turtle round trip (TRT) principle

As you must have discovered already, the TRT principle states that *the Turtle always turns through 360 degrees (or its multiple, such as 720) if it goes along any path and ends at its starting point with its original orientation.*

Now, like most other principles in the world, the TRT principle has its uses. Here is the use that we are interested in:

We know that a round trip is a closed shape. If we take a trip in which (1) all distances are equal, (2) all turns are also equal, and (3) the turns add up to 360, *we must get a regular polygon* - i.e. a closed shape with all angles and sides equal.

Familiar polygons

Let's make the Turtle take 3 equal turns totaling 360. Each turn will be 360/3 = 120.

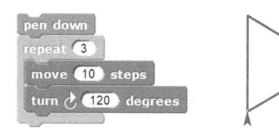

What if we take 4 equal turns that add up to 360? In this case, each turn will be 360/4 = 90. We get a square!

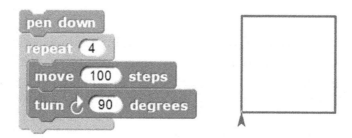

Programming practice

3. Can you extend the above idea to draw a pentagon (a shape with 5 sides) and a hexagon (a shape with 6 sides)? The rules are simple: take identical turns, and all turns must add up to 360.

TRT and polygons

We now have a general idea of how to use the TRT principle to draw any polygon. This idea is stated below.

Important insight

★ A shape consisting of equal length line segments is called a regular polygon. To draw a regular polygon with N sides the Turtle must move forward N times, and turn right by 360/N after each move.

For a triangle, N is 3, so each turn has to be 360/3 = 120.
For a hexagon, N is 6, so each turn has to be 360/6 = 60.

By the way, since Snap provides operators to calculate, we could act lazy and use the script to do all the calculations too. So, an octagon can be drawn with the script:

```
pen down
repeat 8
    move 100 steps
    turn ↻ 360 / 8 degrees
```

Programming practice

4. Create a new custom block called *Triangle* with size as input. So, *Triangle 100* would draw an equilateral triangle with each side 100, *Triangle 50* would draw an equilateral triangle with each side 50, and so on.

5. Create new custom blocks with size input for square, pentagon, hexagon, heptagon, etc.

6. Create a new custom block called *Polygon* that takes 2 inputs: one for size, and the other for number of sides. *Polygon 3 100* would draw a triangle of size 100; *Polygon 6 50* would draw a hexagon with size 50, and so on.

7. Draw a collage of these polygons with different sizes.

8. Continue drawing polygons with larger number of sides and see what you get. You may have to reduce the length of each side to ensure the shape fits on the screen.

It's a circle!

Anyone learning Geometry and experimenting with polygon shapes eventually wants to draw a circle. If you took the practice problem #8 above seriously, you probably have found out how to draw a circle.

If we wanted to draw a regular polygon with a large number of sides, say 100, we could do that using the following instruction:

Doesn't it look like a circle?

Geometry tells us that a circle consists of a large (actually infinite) number of tiny line segments.

Larger the number of segments and tinier the segments, the better the circle would look.

Here is a much better-looking circle which is drawn by:

You will agree that this formula of drawing a circle is also very easy to remember. Note that, it is really still a polygon of 360 sides.

Important insight
★ A circle in Snap is a regular polygon with a large number of tiny sides.

Review questions

1. What is the circumference of this circle? (Hint: The circumference would be equal to the distance traveled by the Turtle.)

Programming practice

9. Draw a semi-circle.

10. Draw a waveform of semi-circles.

Circles of different sizes

You must have noticed that the size of the circle (i.e. its circumference) depends on 2 things: the `repeat` count (let's call it RC) and `move` number of steps (let's call it MI).

```
Circumference = RC x MI
```

That means we can change the circumference either by changing RC or MI. But, as per the TRT principle, changing RC would require us to also change the turn angle (input to `turn`) since the total of all turns must remain 360.

It's much easier to keep RC constant (360) and vary MI to get circles of different circumference as shown in the figure below:

Circumference 360   Circumference 720   Circumference 180

Programming practice

11. Using the discussion above, create a custom block called Circle.C with circumference as input. For example:

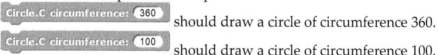

should draw a circle of circumference 360.

should draw a circle of circumference 100.

With diameter as input:

What kind of circle would fit in this square box of size 200? Will our `Circle.C` custom block defined above work here?

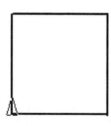

It won't, because ![Circle.C circumference: 200] will draw a circle whose *circumference* is 200. What we need is a circle whose *width* (i.e. diameter) is 200. We need a custom block that can draw a circle of diameter 200 to fit in the square above.

To solve this problem, we tap into our Geometry expertise. We know that for a circle:

```
Circumference = 3.14159 x Diameter
```

(The number 3.14159 above is famous in Mathematics by the name Pi.)

Using this formula, we can convert diameter into circumference and pass it to our circle procedure above.

So:

 will draw a circle of diameter 200.

Circle.C circumference: (300 × 3.14159) will draw a circle of diameter 300.

Circle.C circumference: (400 × 3.14159) will draw a circle of diameter 400.

And so on.

Can we instead create a new custom block that takes diameter as input?

We just have to replace every reference to circumference by an "equivalent" of circumference, i.e. diameter * Pi.

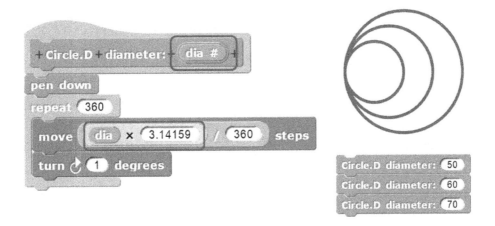

Programming practice

12. The following script draws a triangle. Modify the script to draw a sitting triangle as shown below and then create a new custom block called sitting triangle.

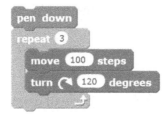 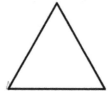

13. Using the Turtle round-trip principle, can you figure out how to draw a five-point star as shown here? (Hint: The Turtle performs a round trip while drawing this star.)

14. Try the same idea for stars with more points. Can you draw stars with 6, 8, 9, or 10 points?

Let's stretch the shapes

Do you know what the main difference between a beautiful drawing and not-so-beautiful drawing is? In other words, what makes a design or shape look nice? Well, we call it "proportions". When an object is *proportionate* it looks nice. Consider the letter E shown below and compare it with the next one:

Chapter 4: Drawing Polygons and Circles

Which one looks better? Do you see what happens when you don't use the right proportions? Do you also see that by *proportions* we mean the *angles* and *proportion of different lengths*?

Important insight

★ A geometric object has two important properties: size and shape. The shape is controlled by angles and proportion of lengths. The size is controlled by the lengths.

So, if we want to zoom into an object (i.e. stretch it), we must change its size but not its shape (i.e. the proportions), otherwise it will look very strange.

So, how do we stretch a design without affecting its shape?

There are two ways to do it as described below.

Fixing one of the dimensions:

In this method, we pick one of the lengths (say height or width) of the object as the "base" and express every other length as a proportion of the "base".

Let's try this idea in an example. We will draw the block L shape as shown below.

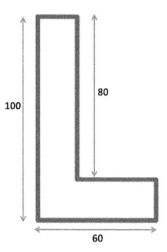

We will create a procedure to draw this shape in 3 flavors (as shown in the figure below): (1) First, we will draw it with fixed values. (2) Next, we will use the shape's height as its "base" dimension and express all others as its multiple. (3) Finally, we will supply the "base" dimension as the procedure's input "h"

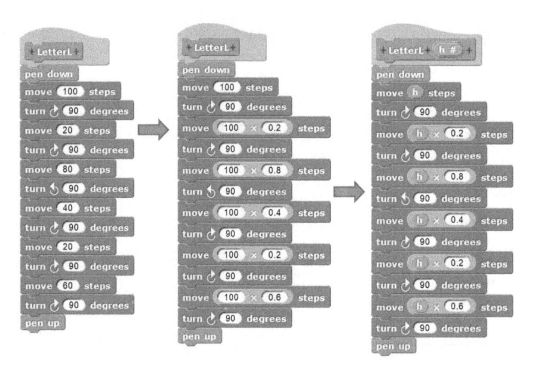

We now just have to supply different values of h as input to to get letter L of different sizes.

Using a scale multiplier:

In this technique, we first draw our shape using actual numbers, and tinker with the numbers until we get the shape in the desired proportion.

Next, we add a "multiplier" to ALL numbers pertaining to dimensions. And make this multiplier our procedure's input.

Example: Let's try this technique on letter F. We will draw the letter with a thick pen to make it appear like a block shape.

As before, we first write the procedure with fixed numbers (no input). Then, we add a multiplier "m" to all dimensions, and make "m" a procedure input.

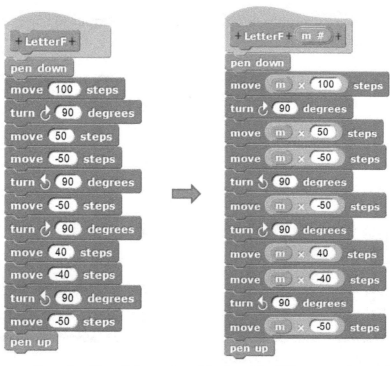

Now, it's a matter of calling this custom block with different values of the scale multiplier.

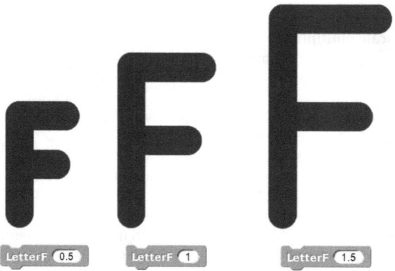

Important insight

★ We saw two methods for stretching (i.e. scaling) designs. In either of them, we do not change any of the angles. That helps us retain their shapes.

Programming practice

15. Try the scaling techniques to draw your favorite English letters with different sizes.

16. Draw the designs shown at the beginning of this chapter.

Review questions

2. The TRT principle can be used to draw PointStars with different number of evenly spaced rays. True or False?

3. To draw a polygon, the Turtle must complete a round trip. True or False?

4. The following script is expected to draw a Heptagon (polygon with 7 sides), but there is a problem as shown below. The polygon is not closing correctly.

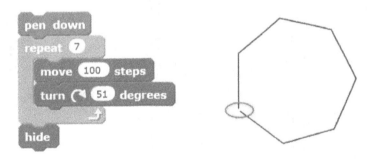

We can fix this problem by:

    a. Changing the input to move to 110.
    b. Changing the repeat count to 7.5.
    c. Changing the turn angle to 360 / 7.
    d. Using a completely different approach.

5. To scale a drawing, we use a scale multiplier for:

a. All `turn` angles
b. All `move` steps
c. All `turn` angles and all `move` steps
d. All the inputs in the script

6. The technique of scaling using a multiplier works only for regular shapes. True or False?

Painting Our Designs:

Introduction

Drawing figures (outlines) usually goes hand in hand with painting, i.e. filling areas with color. And of course, color makes our creative ideas more lively and exciting.

Figure 4-1

In this section, we will learn how to paint shapes in Snap, i.e. how to fill color in our designs to make them look beautiful. And it is quite straightforward. You can then draw pretty designs as shown above.

The FILL Command

Let's say we want to paint our favorite square with the red color. In order to paint this square, the Turtle needs to first jump inside. Note that it has to *jump*, which means it cannot draw a line while getting inside. See Figure A below. Now, the Turtle is ready to paint. Since we want to paint with RED, let's change the brush color to red and then simply call **fill**. See Figure B below.

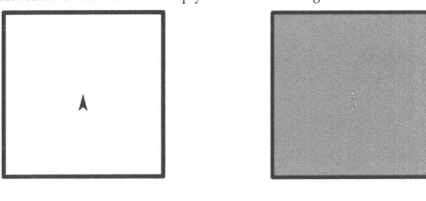

Figure A   Figure B

Important Notes:
- It is essential that the Turtle *jumps* inside the shape, and has no line connecting it with the shape.
- FILL only paints closed shapes. If your shape has an open gap anywhere, FILL will paint the next outer closed shape, or the entire screen!

Playing with FILL:

Let's say we draw the following drawing using the square procedure. If we make the Turtle jump inside the inner square and then call FILL, see what happens.

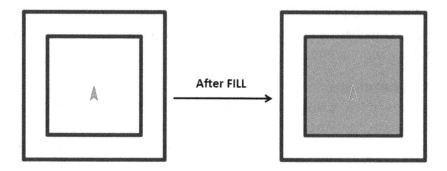

The *nearest closed* shape to the Turtle is the inner square and that's what got painted.

If, on the other hand, we made the Turtle jump inside the space *between* the two squares and then paint, see what happens:

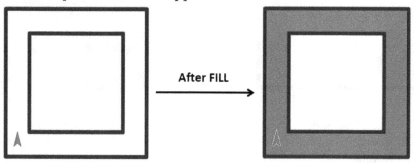

Since the *nearest closed* shape for the Turtle (when FILL is called) is the space between the two squares, that's what got painted.

Note: We will redefine our earlier "Jump" custom block to have 2 inputs: X and Y. Using this block **Jump by x: ⬤ y: ⬤**, the Turtle will move X steps horizontally and Y steps vertically. You will see the actual definition of this block in the next chapter. For now, we will just use it.

The FSquare Procedure

We already have the Square procedure that draws a square of the given `size`.

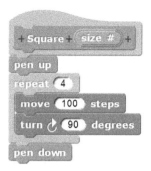

It brings the Turtle to its lower left corner after drawing the square. Let's modify this procedure to draw a painted square.

We need to use the input 'size' not only to draw the square but also to determine *how much* the Turtle should jump in order to paint. We can't use a fixed jump like Jump by x: 50 y: 50 because that would take the Turtle *outside* the square if the square itself were smaller than 50. Do you see the problem?

The easiest way to calculate the jump is to relate it to the 'size' input. So, for example, if the Turtle jumps half as much as 'size', it is guaranteed to stay inside the square. Let's test this idea to ensure it works. We will draw 2 squares side by side.

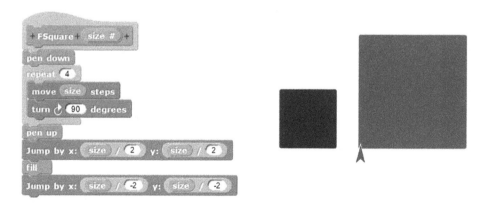

Programming practice:

1. Create the custom block `FTriangle` that draws a painted triangle and takes `size` input.
2. Paint a circle. Create the custom block `FCircle` with `size` input.
3. Paint other shapes that you know, and create interesting designs.
4. Write programs to create the designs shown in Figure 4-1.
5. Create the custom block `FPolygon` that will draw a filled polygon. It will have two inputs: `size` specifying length of each side, and `N` specifying type of polygon.

Chapter 5:
Mirror Images, Flowers, and Other Designs

The first writing of the human being was drawing, not writing.
– Marjane Satrapi

What we will learn in this chapter
- Translation: the idea of moving a shape to a different location.
- Reflection: the idea of creating a mirror image of a shape.
- Rotation: the idea of rotating a shape around a point.
- Drawing complex polygon designs using repetition.
- How to detect the basic polygon shape in complex designs.

Introduction
Using a basic shape (such as a simple square), we can create a lot of entertaining designs by moving it in different ways. Imagine that you have cut out a shape drawn on paper. You could draw its outline by placing it anywhere on a drawing paper. Or, you could flip it along an edge to get a mirror image. Or, you can hold one of its corners with a real pin and rotate it around this pin, while drawing outlines all along to get a flowery pattern.

We will learn how to do these cool things using simple techniques in Snap.

Hopping around
This is the simplest of the possible movements. See below:

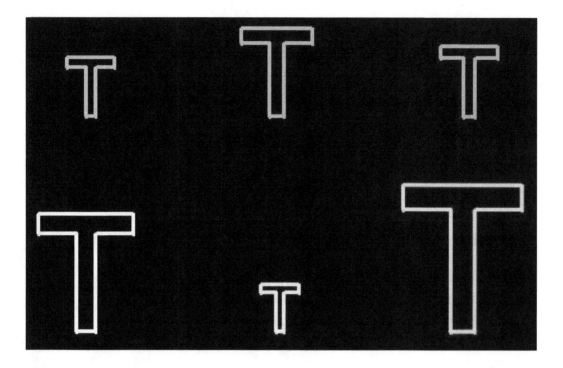

A block T shape has been drawn at various places on the screen. What we want to do is redraw the same shape at different places on the screen without changing its orientation. We can achieve this effect by simply making the Turtle jump to a new location on the screen and then draw the same shape (by running the corresponding script or procedure).

The following script draws two triangles: the Turtle moves 100 steps in the X direction and 50 steps in the Y direction after drawing the first triangle.

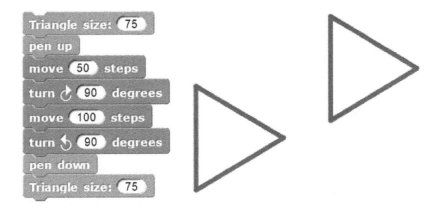

So, as you must have noticed, shifting the Turtle to a new location on the screen is a matter of moving it some distance *up* or *down* and then moving it some distance *left* or *right*.

This type of movement is known in computer graphics as *Translation*.

Programming practice

1. Put the steps of "making the Turtle jump" in a new custom block called Jump. Give it two inputs X and Y. X will specify how much to move left/right and Y will specify how much to move up/down. Jump 100 200 should move the Turtle 100 steps right and 200 steps up. Jump 50 -50 should move the Turtle 50 steps right and 50 steps down.

Using the Jump custom block

Using this new procedure, we can draw our shape anywhere on the screen.

Example:

Programming practice

2. In the above program, use REPEAT and then write a procedure to get any number of squares.

3. Draw multiple instances of your favorite shapes by making the Turtle jump around the screen.

4. Write a program to draw multiple instances of the block letter T on the screen as shown at the beginning of this chapter.

Mirror images

Mirror images (reflections) are very interesting. They are seen in mirrors as well as in still water. (Is there any difference between the two?) In this chapter, we will try to reproduce reflections seen in vertical mirrors.

Let's start with the letter N. It can be drawn using the following script:

```
pen down    ▶ Letter N script
move 100 steps
turn ↻ 135 degrees
move 100 * sqrt ▼ of 2 steps
turn ↺ 135 degrees
move 100 steps
pen up
```

And here is its mirror image and corresponding script:

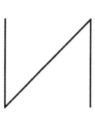

```
pen down    ▶ Mirror image of N
move 100 steps
turn ↺ 135 degrees
move 100 * sqrt ▼ of 2 steps
turn ↻ 135 degrees
move 100 steps
pen up
```

<u>Self-study</u>: Figure out how we came up with the number `100 * (square root of 2)` in the above instruction.

If you compare the two sets of instructions, what do you notice?

We observe that the Turtle motion commands are *identical*, but the turns are exactly *opposite*. `turn ↻` has become `turn ↺` and `turn ↺` has become `turn ↻`.

Let's confirm our hunch by drawing another mirror image.

The following script gives us a triangle.

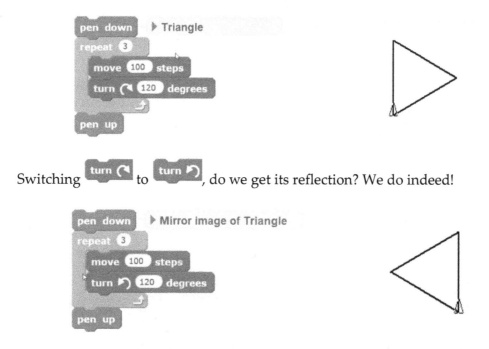

Switching turn ↻ to turn ↺, do we get its reflection? We do indeed!

Important insight

★ To get mirror images (also known as reflections), we simply have to switch all left turns to right turns and right turns to left turns.

Programming practice

5. Create custom blocks for some of your favorite shapes.

6. Create a mirror image custom block for a circle to get the two side-by-side circles below:

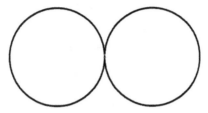

7. The letter F is well suited for mirroring since it is an asymmetric shape. Create custom blocks for a regular block F and for its reflection.

Flowers using rotation

So far, we have seen two types of movements: *translation* and *reflection*. The next one - and probably the most interesting - is *rotation*. This is where we imagine pinning a plastic or paper cut-out of our shape at one of its corners and then rotating it in fixed steps in a clockwise fashion. See the following image.

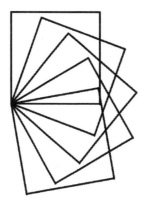

Imagine that we pinned a square at its lower left corner, drew its outline, turned the square by a small angle, and repeated this process 5 times.

Can we draw this kind of design?

First of all, we see that we have to draw a bunch of squares. So, we can make use of our square custom block reproduced below:

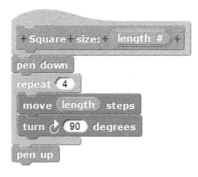

We also know that rotating the paper cut-out is the same as changing the orientation of the Turtle. Let's see what the following instructions give:

    Chapter 5: Mirror Images, Flowers, and Other Designs

So, our hunch is correct! If we do this 5 times we will get the design shown at the beginning of this section.

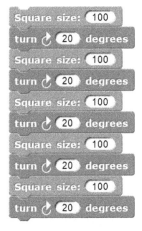

To your keen eyes, does anything obvious appear in the instructions above?

Yes! There clearly is a *repetition* of the same 2 instructions. We can employ our powerful `repeat` command to make this code compact.

What if we wanted a complete flower of squares such that it looks symmetric and beautiful? We will basically have to increase the *count* input of REPEAT. What should this *count* be to create a symmetric and complete flower?

Well, we can apply our *school geometry knowledge* to our advantage. We know that the total angle the Turtle turns through in one complete spin around itself is 360. So, obviously, all we have to do to get a nice-looking complete flower is to ensure that *the total of all turns is 360*. We chose 18 as the input of `repeat` because 18 * 20 = 360. See what we get!

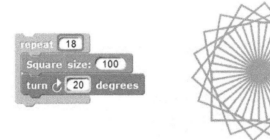

Programming practice

8. Rotate the square shape to get the following designs. Also, try your own designs.

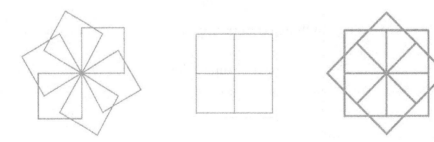

Nested repeat

Instead of using the `Square` custom block, if we had simply used standard Snap blocks, our script to draw a flower of 18 squares would look as follows:

We have used a REPEAT inside another REPEAT. In programming lingo, this is called *nested repeat*. Just for your information!

Since we are calling our designs as flowers, we will call each of its squares as a *petal*.

Programming practice

9. Create a custom block called SqFlower (short for flower of squares) that takes 2 inputs: size of each square and number of petals. So, for example:

   SqFlower 100 5 should draw a flower of 5 squares each of size 100
   SqFlower 50 20 should draw a flower of 20 squares each of size 50

10. Replace the square with a triangle and draw various types of triangle flowers: dumb-bell (2 petals), fan (4 petals), and so on.

  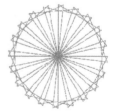

11. Draw flowers of other polygon shapes: pentagon, hexagon, etc.

Nested blocks

Our triangle custom block is as given below:

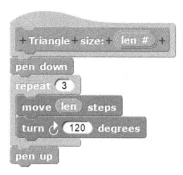

And, as we just learned above, here is how we can draw flowery patterns of triangles:

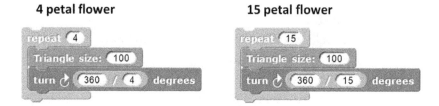

We could write a new procedure called TriFlower that is capable of drawing any flower of triangles. It would have 2 inputs: size of each triangle, and the number of triangles (petals).

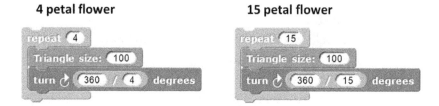

So, will draw a 4-petal flower.

And `TriFlower size: 50 petals 18` will draw an 18-petal flower.

The purpose of showing this example is to demonstrate to you that we can use our *new custom blocks* just like Snap *blocks*, even in a nested way: the new `TrFlower` custom block in turn uses our other custom block called `Triangle`.

Review questions

1. What is Translation?
    a. It is the act of turning an object around its center.
    b. It is the act of moving an object from one place to another without changing its orientation and size.
    c. It is the act of resizing an object without changing its location.
    d. It is the act of changing the object's name from one language to another.

2. To get a mirror image of an object:
    a. We need to reverse the direction of every turn.
    b. We need to make all turns to left turns.
    c. We need to make all turns to right turns.
    d. We need to rotate the object by 180 degrees.

3. If we want to draw a perfect flower of 36 squares, how much should the Turtle turn after drawing each square?
    a. 36 degrees
    b. 20 degrees
    c. 10 degrees
    d. 5 degrees

4. The following design is drawn by repeating a basic shape 10 times. What shape is that?

    a. Square
    b. Cube
    c. Parallelogram
    d. Pentagon

Programming practice

12. Draw flowers of circles. Examples are shown below:

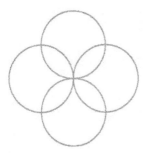 

13. The idea of a flower of circles can be extended to draw the design shown below. (Does it look a bit like our Earth with its hot core? Well, maybe!):

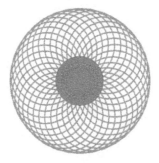

14. You must have seen the following optical illusion in puzzle books. It has a 3-D feel to it. See if you can draw this using our idea of rotation.

15. Draw a row of squares using the repeat command.

16. Can you draw the Olympic logo shown below?

17. Create custom blocks that show the Sun and a total solar eclipse, i.e. a drawing that consists of a dark circle and spikes emanating from it.

18. Create a general-purpose flower custom block called "Polygon.Flower" that will draw a flower of any polygon. It will take 3 inputs: type of polygon i.e. number of sides, number of petals and size of each petal.

Insights and tips

- REPEAT is not just a handy little command that saves typing; amazing new possibilities open up that would be impossible without REPEAT. (Imagine drawing a flower of circles without the help of REPEAT).
- Before using REPEAT, you must first figure out the repeated basic pattern, which may consist of a visible pattern (lines) and an invisible pattern (angles and gaps).
- To figure out the basic pattern in a complicated design, simply trace the motion of Turtle from the central point of the design and note all lines and turns. Remember, in a regular polygon, all lines and turns must be equal.
- Programming allows infinite experimentation - so don't be afraid to try out your ideas and hunches. If they turn out to be incorrect (weird stuff gets drawn on the screen), either pat yourself on the back for amazing new discoveries (if the weird stuff looks pretty) or go back to your notebook, make changes, and try again.
- Do not forget to solve the problem in your mind (and notebook) first, before writing Snap programs. Remember that Snap is not going to help you solve the problem; it will simply replicate all the mistakes that you have made yourself in your design.

Chapter 6:
Problem-solving Using Divide and Conquer

The secret of getting ahead is getting started. The secret of getting started is breaking your complex overwhelming tasks into small manageable tasks, and starting on the first one. – Mark Twain

What we will learn in this chapter
- The idea that a complex problem can be solved by breaking it down into multiple smaller, simpler problems.
- Programming process: design, scripting (coding), testing, and debugging.

Introduction
We have been learning a lot of little tricks of programming so far and applying them to write lots of little programs. Now, we are ready to write some "seriously cool" programs. See the collage below. Each of the figures is an interesting combination of multiple shapes.

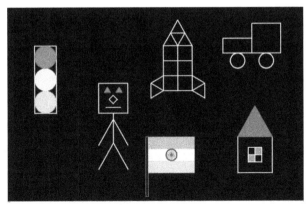

Figure 6.1

Before you start churning out programs for these fancy objects, let's take a couple of simple examples and understand the process of how to go about developing such programs.

Block arrow

Consider the figure shown here. Let's say we want to write a script to draw this block arrow.

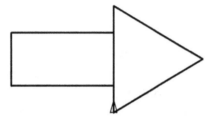

One way is to just start drawing at some point and go around to finish it off. We call it "connect-the-dots" technique.

Connect the dots

The block arrow above is a simple enough drawing that we can draw by using the *connect-the-dots* approach. In the image shown next, we have numbered the important dots.

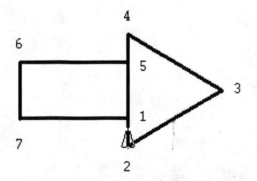

If we imagine that our Turtle is at position 1 to begin with, we can move it along the path 1-2-3-4-5-6-7-1-5-2 to complete the picture. Here is the script to do that:

```
pen down
move -25 steps
turn ↻ 60 degrees        move 100 steps
move 100 steps           turn ↺ 90 degrees
turn ↺ 120 degrees       move 50 steps
move 100 steps           turn ↺ 90 degrees
turn ↺ 120 degrees       move 100 steps
move 25 steps            turn ↺ 90 degrees
turn ↻ 90 degrees        move 50 steps
                         move -75 steps
```

As little children, all of us have used this approach to solve puzzles in which there were mystery figures to be discovered. And this may also sound like a reasonable way to create the drawing script.

But, there are many problems in this approach. First, can you draw block arrows of *any size* using this approach? Second, can you imagine using this approach to draw a *rocket* or the *flag* (as shown in the collage above)?

It would be *ridiculously complicated*.

We need a better technique. There is, in fact, a much smarter way to draw such drawings, and it is called *Divide and Conquer*.

Divide and conquer

In this approach, we take a step back (or forward, if you prefer!) and take a careful look at the design and ask the question, "What is this design made up of? Can we break it up into separate parts that are meaningful and reusable?"

Certainly, when you ask this question for the block arrow above, the obvious answer is: "Yes, we see two parts: a *rectangle* and an *equilateral triangle*."

At this point, we do not worry about actual dimensions (sizes) of these components.

The next step is to go about designing each of these components *separately*.

We know from experience that a *rectangle* is drawn by the following custom block. The inputs 'h' and 'w' determine the *height* and *width* of the rectangle respectively. We test this custom block (by giving various inputs) to make sure it works.

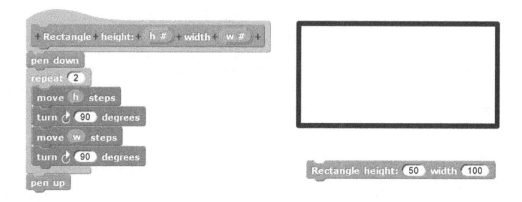

And an *equilateral triangle* is drawn by the following custom block. The input 'size' determines the *length* of each side. We test this custom block (by giving various inputs) to make sure it works.

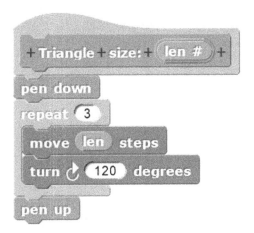

Now, it's just a matter of *putting these components together* to get the block arrow. But, to do that, we need to do some *design* work in our notebook. We basically have to go through the following decision-making process. The answers (decisions) shown are part arbitrary and part based on some mental analysis of the shapes and their dimensions.

1. In what order should we draw the components? - *The decision in this case is: first the rectangle and then triangle.*

2. How big should the rectangle be? - *We decide that height = 50, width = 100*

3. How big should the triangle be? - *We decide that size = 100*

4. How should we position the Turtle to draw the triangle? - *We need to move the Turtle (without drawing anything) to the point labeled 2 in the connect-the-dots figure shown earlier.*

With these answers, we can write the script for the block arrow:

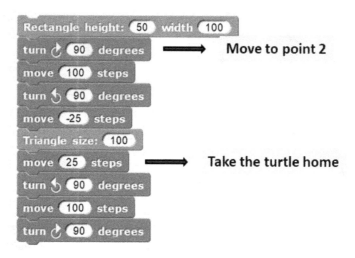

Next, we put this script into a new custom block called `Block.Arrow`. Once again, we will test this custom block to make sure it works.

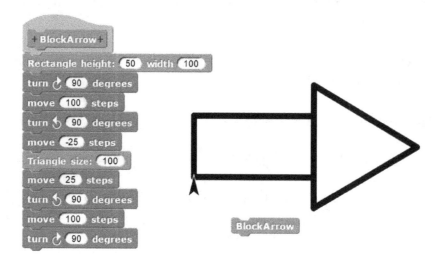

And finally, we will add a scaling factor (the input "m") to allow us to draw a block arrow of any size. Let us test this custom block to make sure it works:

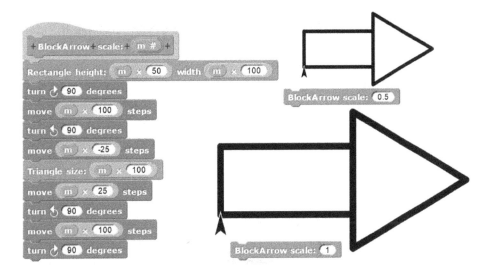

We are done!

Divide-and-conquer may seem like a lengthy process, but it really isn't. It seems that way because we are using it for the first time. The beauty of this approach, in fact, is that there is very little room for making mistakes, and the components can be used for other designs also.

Review questions
1. Using the above custom block, how will you draw block arrows pointing in other directions, such as, North or South?

Programming practice
1. Draw a collage of block arrows of different sizes, pointing in different directions, and of different colors and thickness.

Another example: House
Let's go through another interesting example to make sure we understand the *divide-and-conquer* method. We will attempt to draw the house as shown here.

First, we take a step back and take a keen look at the design and ask the standard question:

"What is this design made up of? Can we break it apart into meaningful reusable components or parts?"

We come up with the answer: "Yes, we see three parts: a *wall,* a *roof,* and a *window.*"

  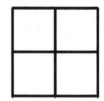

At this stage, we will not worry about actual dimensions (sizes) of these components.

The next step is to go about designing these components separately.

We see that the *wall* is just a plain *square*. So, creating a custom block for the wall is straightforward. First, we create a custom block "Square". The input 'size' determines the *length* of each side. And next, we create the `wall` custom block (it will simply use the `Square` custom block).

We test this custom block (by giving various inputs) to make sure it works.

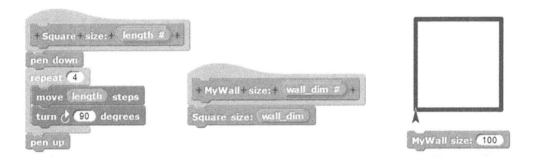

The roof is also easy: it is a *sitting equilateral triangle*. The input 'size' determines the *length* of each side. In a previous chapter, we have learnt how to draw a triangle in different positions.

We test this custom block (by giving various inputs) to make sure it works.

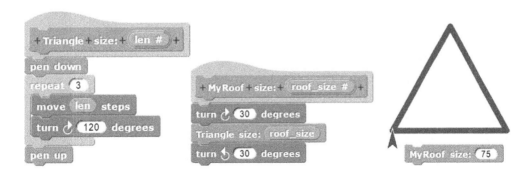

Next, we need to draw the window. If you remember "polygon rotation", the window looks like a small square rotated 4 times. We will put this script into a custom block called `MyWindow`. The input 'pane_size' will control the *size* of each square.

We test this custom block (by giving various inputs) to make sure it works.

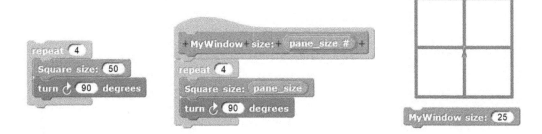

So, we are done with all individual components.

Now, it's just a matter of *putting these components together* to get the *house*. But, to do that, we need to do some *design* work in our notebook. We basically have to go through the following decision-making process:

1. In what order should we draw the components? – *First the wall, then the window, and then the roof.* (Note: the sequence is entirely up to us, we can draw in any order)

2. Determine sizes of each component. *We decide that:*
    a. *Wall size = 100*
    b. *Roof size = 100*
    c. *Window (each little square) size = 25*

3. How should we position the Turtle to draw the window? - *We need to move the Turtle (without drawing anything) to the center of the wall.*

4. How should we position the Turtle to draw the roof? - *We need to move the Turtle (without drawing anything) above the wall.*

With all these answers, we are ready to write the script for the house:

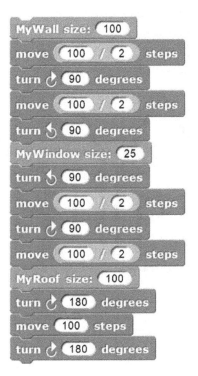

Next, we will put this script into a new custom block called MyHouse. Once again, we will test this custom block to make sure it works. And finally, we will add a scaling factor (the input "m") to allow us to draw a house of any size. Let us test this custom block to make sure it works. We will use our Jump custom block to draw 3 houses in a row.

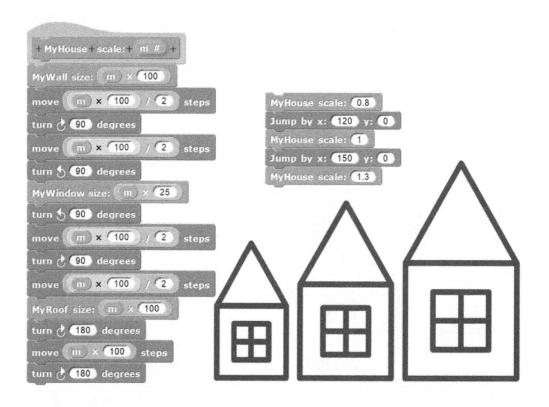

Programming practice

2. Draw a collage of houses of different sizes, colors, and thickness.
3. Do you feel you are now ready to draw some of the interesting designs in the collage shown in Figure 6.1? Just follow the divide-and-conquer method and you will have no problems.
4. Draw any other cool designs that you can think of which might benefit from the divide-and-conquer approach.

Chapter 7:
Drawing Curvy Objects

I've always been amazed by Da Vinci, because he worked out science on his own. He would work by drawing things and writing down his ideas. He designed all sorts of flying machines way before you could actually build something like that. – Bill Gates

What we will learn in this chapter
- Drawing interesting curves using a quarter circle.
- Application of the TRT principle.
- How to draw "irregular" shapes (like a rock or a grass blade).

Introduction
With the exception of circles, we have so far only seen how to draw designs that contain straight lines. We don't know yet how to draw nice curvy objects like a lotus flower, a flying bird, or a fish. Or a beautiful garden as shown below:

In this chapter, we will discover that we can draw curves without needing to learn anything new; not even new Turtle commands. We will see that it's all just the magic of simple geometry.

So, let's get on with it.

Circle as our starting point

Since we already know how to draw one type of curve, i.e. a circle, we will start from there:

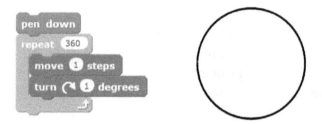

We also understand how we get the circle: As the Turtle takes 360 tiny steps and turns 1 degree at every step, we get a circle. The Turtle returns home because it turns through a total of 360 degrees (TRT principle).

As we worked out previously, the procedures for circles of any size are:

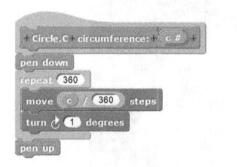

Now, if we wanted to draw a semi-circle, what would we have to do? Think a moment before reading on.

How to draw a semi-circle

Clearly, a semi-circle is *half* the work of drawing a full circle. So, if we ask the Turtle to stop *half-way*, wouldn't we get a semi-circle? Let's try.

To stop half-way we should ask the Turtle to take 180 steps instead of 360, keeping everything else the same.

We do indeed get a semi-circle!

The procedures for drawing semi-circles would derive easily from the circle procedures by just replacing the repeat count 360 with 180.

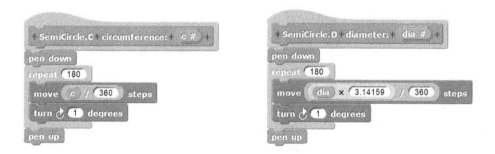

Note that input 'c' specifies the circumference of the *full circle*. So, the length of the semi-circle would be c/2.

Let's test these procedures to draw a bunch of semi-circles.

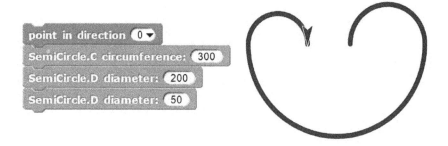

Do you see the 3 semi-circles that we drew one after the other?

Programming practice
1. Using the semi-circle procedures draw different designs of your liking.
2. Draw the rainbow design as shown below.

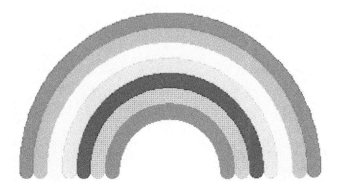

Drawing a quarter circle
Now that we have figured out half circle, why not try a quarter circle? It turns out that it's not just a whim that we are satisfying by doing this, but the quarter circle is actually quite a nifty little thing. It is a basic building block for many interesting drawings.

So, let' see how to get a quarter circle. We stopped at 180 degrees to get a half circle, so you can easily guess where we or rather the Turtle needs to stop to draw a quarter circle.

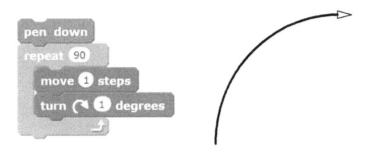

This is our so-called quarter circle. It doesn't appear very special as yet, but wait to see its hidden powers.

The procedures for drawing quarter circles would derive easily from the circle procedures just by replacing the repeat count 360 with 90.

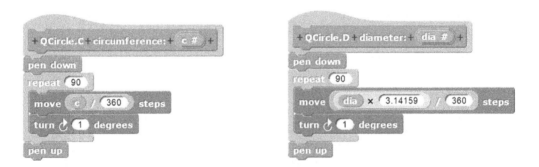

Note that input 'c' of QCircle.C specifies the circumference of the *full circle*. So, the actual length of the quarter circle would be c/4.

Note also that input 'dia' of QDcircle.D specifies the diameter of the *full circle*.

Let's test these procedures to draw a bunch of quarter circles.

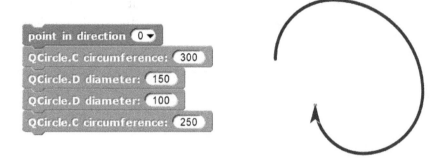

Do you see the 4 quarter circles drawn one after the other?

Programming practice

3. Can you draw a semi-circle and a full circle just using quarter circles?

4. Can you figure out how to draw the quarter circle shown here?

Fun with the Quarter Circle

As we hinted earlier, a lot of different things can be done with the quarter circle. See this shape:

Can you figure out how it is drawn?

Clearly, there are 2 quarter circles. But, in between there is a turn that the Turtle has to take. If you are not sure what the turn is, try different values.

The above *petal* (that's what we will call it) can be drawn using:

```
point in direction 0 ▾
QCircle.D diameter: 100
turn ↻ 90 degrees
QCircle.D diameter: 100
turn ↻ 90 degrees
```

The last turn is not required for the petal, but we have added it to bring the Turtle back to its original state.

Here is the Petal procedure. The size input is the diameter of the full circle.

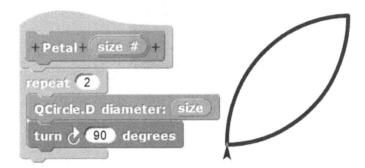

As you can see, the petal is tilted to the right. Can you use the procedure above in a way to get an exactly vertical petal?

The median of the petal would be at half the angle of the right turn (i.e. 45). So, in order to get a symmetric petal around the Turtle's present orientation, we should tilt the Turtle to the left by 45 before drawing the petal.

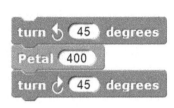 

Programming practice

5. Draw a candle as shown below.

6. Draw various designs using the petal as shown below:

7. How about a plant? Write a "plant" procedure.

8. Using the plant procedure written above, draw a garden similar to the one shown at the beginning of this chapter.

Exploring the quarter circle further

While drawing a petal, we drew a quarter circle and then took a *right* turn before drawing the second quarter circle.

What would happen if the Turtle took a *left* turn instead?

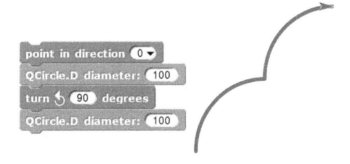

Does it look like a flying bird?

Programming practice

9. The bird above is tilted at an angle. Can you draw it flat, i.e. flying parallel to the ground?

Something fishy:

In order to draw a petal, we drew a quarter circle, took a **90** degree turn, and then drew the second quarter circle. Can you think of modifying this idea just a bit to get the fish below?

Clearly, the Turtle needs to turn a bit more than 90 degrees before drawing the second quarter circle. The following instructions draw a fish.

Programming practice

10. Can you create this chain of fish holding hands (or fins)?

11. The fish drawn earlier is tilted at an angle. Can you draw it flat, i.e. swimming parallel to the ground?

12. How about a fish with a proper tail?

13. The following pattern consists of 4 quarter circles. Check it out. (<u>Hint</u>: Think about using the TRT principle.)

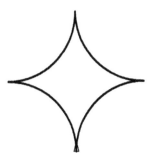

14. How about this next one?

<u>Hint</u>: Once again you can use the TRT principle with a bit of arithmetic.

15. Now that you have figured out the above two designs, work out a similar design with 8 arcs (and 9, 10, 12, and so on).

Making waves

In a previous chapter we were able to draw waves using semi-circles. We can do the same using quarter circles. We will need two kinds of quarter circle. We will need a separate quarter circle that draws anti-clockwise:

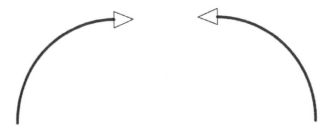

Here are the procedures for drawing anti-clockwise:

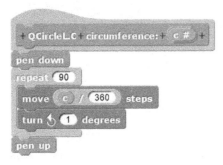

Quarter circle anti-clockwise
Input is circumference

```
QCircleL.C  circumference: c #
pen down
repeat 90
  move  c / 360  steps
  turn ↺ 1 degrees
pen up
```

Quarter circle anti-clockwise
Input is diameter

```
QCircleL.D  diameter: dia #
pen down
repeat 90
  move  dia × 3.14159 / 360  steps
  turn ↺ 1 degrees
pen up
```

Using a combination of *right* quarter circle and *left* quarter circle we can create a nice looking wave:

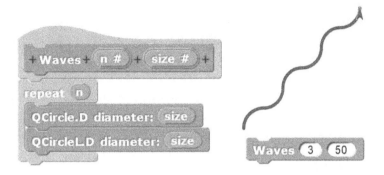

Programming practice

16. Make the wave above appear horizontal.

17. The figure below shows the leaf pattern of a Chestnut tree. The amazing thing is that all Chestnut leaves appear in the exact same pattern as shown: always in groups of 7 with one large leaf at the top, and remaining 6 appearing as mirror images. <u>Hint</u>: First write a procedure to draw an individual leaf (use a 'size' input to control the size of the leaf). Then, design the full pattern.

18. Design the pair of eyes as shown below: Any comments needed?

19. Can you make a snake go around a stick?

Drawing irregular curves

So far we have only been playing with circles and parts of circles. But, as you know, not all curves in the world are as "regular" as circles. See the rock below for example:

Clearly, it would be very difficult to draw this rock just with quarter circles.

But, if we use pieces of circles (called *arcs*) that are of variety of lengths, we could put them together to get all kinds of curves. The rock above, for example, is drawn by the instructions below. **Please note** that it is really one single script split into 2 scripts just for the sake of convenient viewing!

```
pen down
point in direction (0▾)
repeat (100)
    move (1) steps
    turn ↻ (1) degrees
repeat (50)
    move (1) steps
    turn ↺ (1) degrees
repeat (50)
    move (1) steps
    turn ↻ (1) degrees
```

```
move (50) steps
repeat (75)
    move (1) steps
    turn ↻ (1) degrees
repeat (23)
    move (1) steps
    turn ↺ (1) degrees
pen up
```

We even have a bit of flat surface (for us to sit and watch the sunrise!) on this rock (drawn by `move (50) steps`). We really have to experiment with the sections to design a rock of our liking.

So, that's really the key to draw curves of irregular shapes. Just take the Turtle on random travel (using circle sections and straight lines as desired).

You can convert the above script into a "Rock" procedure.

And here are the instructions to draw the picture as shown above:

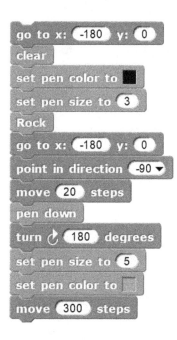

Review questions

1. A circle in Snap:
    a. Is a polygon with a large number of sides.
    b. Is impossible to draw because TRT principle fails for a circle.
    c. Is drawn by using the "circle" command block.
    d. Can only be drawn in the Paint editor.

2. The TRT principle can be used to draw irregular curves because:
    a. Irregular curves are a type of regular polygons.
    b. Irregular curves are combinations of multiple circles.
    c. TRT works for any closed shape, whether it is curved or not.
    d. The sum of all turns comes to 180.

3. What will the following script draw?

   a. A semi-circle
   b. A full circle
   c. 2 unconnected semi-circles
   d. 3 quarters of a circle

4. What is the circumference of the circle drawn by the following script?

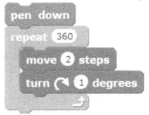

   a. 360
   b. 180
   c. 720
   d. 100

5. If "qcircle" draws a quarter circle, what will the following script draw?

   a. A semi-circle
   b. 8 unconnected quarter circles
   c. A full circle
   d. 2 circles

Programming practice

20. See if you can draw the wavy grass below:

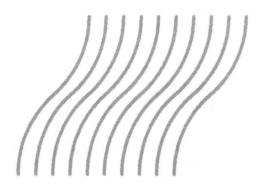

Hint: You just need to work out how to draw one blade. Then, it's a matter of using REPEAT.

21. On similar lines, you could try the wavy water pattern shown below:

Chapter 8:
Power of Polygons

It's not what you look at that matters, it's what you see. – Alphonso Dunn

What we will learn in this chapter
- Extending polygons
- Doing excursions before drawing a polygon
- Drawing polygon patterns as excursions while drawing the base polygon
    - Pattern outside the base polygon
    - Pattern inside the base polygon
    - Pattern larger than the side of the base polygon
    - Pattern smaller than the side of the base polygon
    - Hiding the base polygon
- Rotating random patterns to create polygonal designs
- Drawing polygons around their center and associated designs

Introduction
Earlier, we used our knowledge of geometry to draw interesting but simple designs using regular polygons. We will explore this idea further and develop some expertise in this very exciting field of "Geometric Designs".

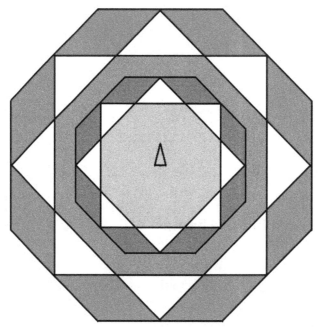

Figure 8.1

You must have seen patterns - like the one shown here - used for tiles, cutlery, architectures, and even paintings. All that we really need to know to create such designs is polygons, Turtle Round Trip principle, and the Turtle commands that we already know. Are you interested? Then, read on.

Teaching the Turtle to play mischief

We have learnt in the Turtle Round Trip theorem that the Turtle turns through 360 degrees (or its multiple) whenever it goes around the screen and ends up at the same starting position and orientation.

We have used this knowledge to create regular polygons (shapes whose internal angles and edges are identical).

So how can we draw a shape shown here?

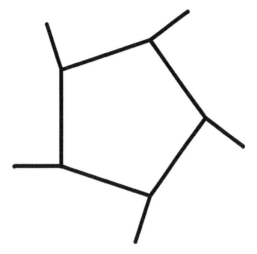

Let us analyze the shape. There is a pentagon (5-sided polygon) and there is a line that extends from each of its vertices. Let's call this line a "whisker".

A simple pentagon is drawn by:

```
pen down
repeat 5
    move 100 steps
    turn ↻ 360 / 5 degrees
```

We can draw the "whisker" by turning left, drawing a short line, and then turning right again to continue drawing the pentagon:

```
pen down
repeat 5
    turn ↺ 90 degrees
    move 50 steps
    move -50 steps
    turn ↻ 90 degrees
    move 100 steps
    turn ↻ 360 / 5 degrees
```

This is just as if the Turtle is playing a little *mischief on the side* while performing the main task of drawing the pentagon.

Can we use this 'mischief' idea and have the Turtle give us the following design? This time the mischief involves drawing a full rectangle on top of each side of the pentagon.

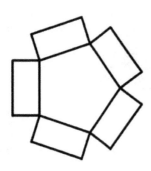

```
pen down
repeat 5
    move 100 steps        ▶ Start mischief
    turn ↺ 90 degrees
    move 50 steps
    turn ↺ 90 degrees
    move 100 steps
    turn ↺ 90 degrees
    move 50 steps
    turn ↺ 90 degrees
    move 100 steps        ▶ Draw pentagon
    turn ↻ 360 / 5 degrees
```

Important insight

★ We get interesting designs by making the Turtle take a side trip while
   drawing a regular polygon. The important part is to get the Turtle back to
   its original position and direction (to make it appear as if the Turtle did not
   do anything!)

We can now go one step ahead and make the pentagon invisible.

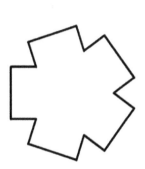

```
pen down
repeat 5
    pen up          ▶ Start mischief. Hide first side
    move 100 steps
    pen down
    turn ↺ 90 degrees
    move 100 steps
    turn ↺ 90 degrees
    move 50 steps
    turn ↺ 90 degrees
    pen up          ▶ Hide pentagon
    move 100 steps   ▶ Draw pentagon
    pen down
    turn ↻ 360 / 5 degrees
```

Self-study: Modify the code written earlier and draw the same figure using the
`Rectangle` custom block. Hint: Think of another way of making the pentagon
disappear!

Programming practice

1. Create a custom block PStar that will draw a polygon star (number of
   sides and size provided as input). One example is shown here:

<u>Hint</u>: The mischief this time will involve drawing an equilateral triangle and then making the polygon invisible.

Polygons in and out: Super-polygons

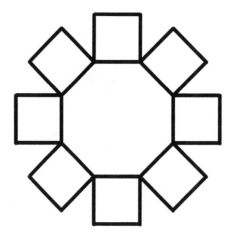

What will we need to do to draw a figure shown here? We see two regular polygons - an octagon at the center and a square on each side of the octagon.

We get the regular octagon using

```
pen down
repeat 8
    move 75 steps
    turn ↻ 360 / 8 degrees
```

And we can get the above design by drawing a square before drawing the side of the octagon. Note the change of Turtle orientation before and after drawing the square.

```
pen down
repeat 8
    turn ↺ 90 degrees
    repeat 4
        move 75 steps
        turn ↻ 90 degrees
    turn ↻ 90 degrees
    move 75 steps
    turn ↻ 360 / 8 degrees
```

We can use the generic Polygon custom block we created earlier, to draw the Square.

```
pen down
repeat 8
    turn ↺ 90 degrees
    Polygon edges: 4  75
    turn ↻ 90 degrees
    move 75 steps
    turn ↻ 360 / 8 degrees
```

Programming practice

2. Can you eliminate the need to turn left first in the figure above? <u>Hint</u>: Draw the polygon using left turns (instead of right turns).

Important insight

★ We can draw a polygon shape on the outside of a polygon to create Super-polygons. Both these polygons must share a side of the same length.

Programming practice

3. Create a custom block Super.Polygon to draw the following designs. It should have following inputs.

a. N.in = Number of sides of the inside polygon
b. N.out = Number of sides of the outside polygon
c. Size = Size of the inside polygon

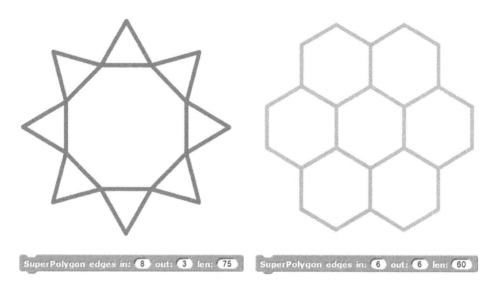

Reversing sides
What will we need to do to draw a figure shown below?

What if you were told that this figure is related to the next figure in some way? Clearly, the outside octagon has been made to hide.

But, how do we get the following figure in the first place?

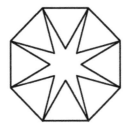

Here is the code that will produce the design.

```
pen down
repeat 8
    PolygonR edges: 3  75    ——→ Draws the inside triangle
    move 75 steps
    turn ↻ 360 / 8 degrees
```

It's really the same idea as before, except this time, the triangle is drawn on the inside of the main octagon.

You could get rid of the octagon in the following way: avoid drawing it in the first place – this will require you to create a new custom Polygon block that does not draw the base edge. See below:

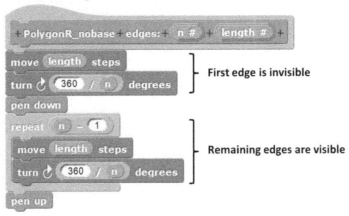

Programming practice

    4. Create a custom block Super.Polygon.In (one which draws the extra polygon inside) to create the following designs.

Hint: First, look for the base polygon (in the above examples, it's the outermost invisible polygon), count its number of sides, and then figure out (just by visual inspection) what kind of second polygon is to be drawn on the inside for each. (For the first one, it's a square.)

Important insight

  ★ We can create different Super-polygons when we change the basic pattern on the inside of the base polygon. Erasing the base polygon makes it even more interesting.

Polygons without edges

So far, we explored a technique in which we first ask the Turtle to draw a regular polygon (we call it the "base" polygon). Next, while drawing the main polygon we teach the Turtle to play a "sideways mischief" of drawing another polygon either outside or inside the base polygon.

In theory, the extra polygon need not be a polygon at all; it could be any random design. Also, we could ignore the "base polygon" altogether. That is, we need not even bother to draw the sides of the base polygon.

See the following example that combines these two adventures:
We will try the spike figure below as our side-design (instead of a regular polygon).

The two sides are of the same length (let's call it D) and they make the same angle with the X-axis (i.e. the ground). Let's call this angle X.

So, to draw this shape, the Turtle would do the following:

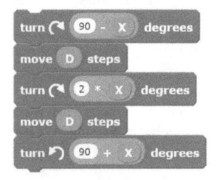

This can be put into a custom block format by making X and D inputs:

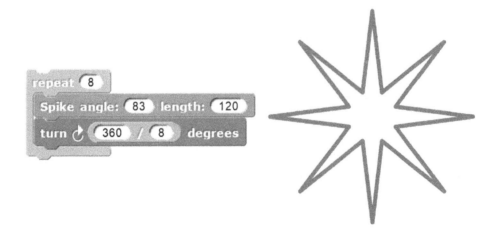

Now, using the Spike as a side, we will create an octagon of spikes and see what we get.

This indeed looks like the earlier star figure.

Programming practice

5. Using the Spike custom block, write scripts to draw the following designs.

6. In place of spikes the following designs use other novel shapes (as noted beneath each figure). Can you work out the script for each?

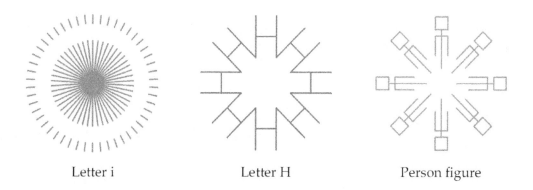

Letter i   Letter H   Person figure

Important insight

★ Any pattern can be rotated through a 360 degree turn to create a polygonal design. If the base pattern shifts the Turtle sideways while retaining its orientation, we get a polygon with the pattern on the side. Otherwise we get a point-star like design.

Irregular sides

(This section is based on material from Prof. Brian Harvey's Logo Book Vol 1).

So far we have used fairly regular and geometrically balanced shapes to create super polygons. Do you think we should try using any random pattern as a side of a polygon? Consider the following pattern called "squiggle":

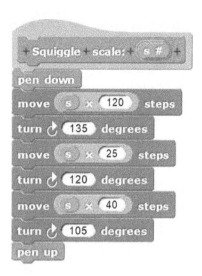

We will just rotate this squiggle pattern such that the total turn angle is 360 degrees as suggested by the TRT principle. (We will call this the *hidden polygon technique* since there is no real polygon being drawn.)

Examples:

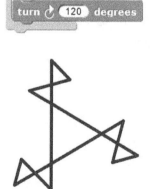

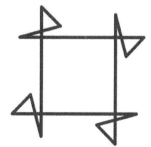

<u>Note</u>: For this to work, the instructions to draw the basic pattern should retain the Turtle's original heading, i.e. we expect the total turn within the basic pattern to be 360 or its multiple.

Programming practice

7. Create an irregular pattern of your own and try rotating it!

Rings of polygons

Let's continue our exploration of interesting polygon designs, shall we? Can you visualize the basic pattern used in the figure below?

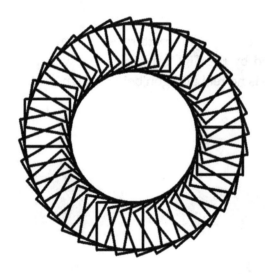

You guessed it right – it is a ring of squares. It appears to be rotated along a circle. However, we know that a circle is nothing but a polygon with many sides!

This is simply a little variation on the "Polygon on the inside" approach. A simple 36-side polygon has been modified by inserting a square shape.

The following script will draw this design:

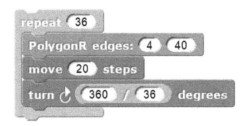

Here is a bit of explanation: The outside REPEAT loop makes the sprite move along a polygon of 36 edges, but without drawing it (since pen is up). At every edge we draw a square, and thus get the above design.

Go ahead and experiment with this script. See what you get if you draw squares of different sizes – smaller than 20 or bigger.

Programming practice

8. Using a similar approach, write instructions to draw the following ring designs.

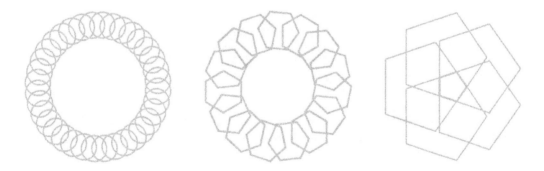

Drawing polygons with Turtle at the center

So far, as you might have noticed, our Turtle has been drawing regular polygons by staying on their perimeter. This is a little inconvenient if we want to draw concentric designs, i.e. designs that are drawn around a point.

Imagine, for example, drawing a hexagon and then a smaller square inside the hexagon such that the two shapes are exactly centered.

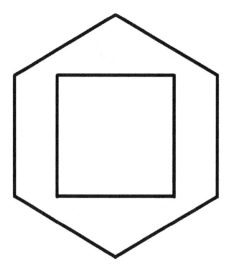

You might think the following instructions would do the job. In this script, we draw the outer hexagon, shift the Turtle to the right, and draw the square.

```
PolygonR edges: 6  100
Jump by x: 20  y: 0
PolygonR edges: 4  100
```

But, how do we know how much the Turtle needs to move before drawing the square? Calculating that would be too complicated, and if we guess, our guess may not be correct.

Instead, we could figure out how to draw each of these polygons such that the Turtle stays at their center. Then, all designs would be concentric automatically!

We will explore this idea for some of the common polygons and try to draw them around their center point. For the rest of them, it's homework for you!

Square around its center

This can be done in 3 simple steps: (1) Move the Turtle to the lower left corner of the (would-be) square, (2) Draw the square using our generic polygon custom block, (3) Move the Turtle back to the center.

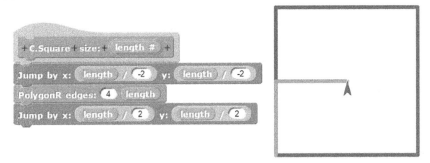

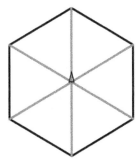 will draw a square around the present location.

Hexagon around its center

See the hexagon below. The center point has 6 identical equilateral triangles around it.

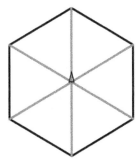

The hexagon can be drawn in 3 simple steps:

1. Move the Turtle to the top corner of the (would-be) hexagon and turn right 120,
2. Draw the hexagon the old-fashioned way, and

3. Move the Turtle back to the center.

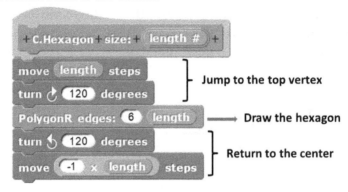

C.Hexagon size: 150 will draw a hexagon around a center point.

Octagon around its center

The octagon is slightly complicated (but fun!). See the figure below:

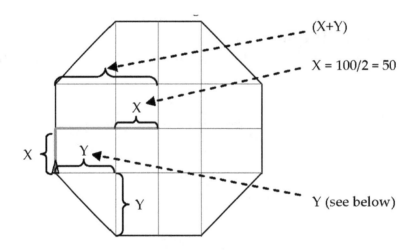

Let's say the length L of each edge of the hexagon is 100.

The thick line shows how we need to move the Turtle from the center, to be able to use our usual method to draw the octagon. The challenge is to figure out the lengths of these two moves. The second move (X) is straightforward: it's L/2.

The first move consists of two parts X and Y. We know X already (L/2). We can compute Y using the Pythagoras formula (since Y is part of a right-angle triangle in the figure). This gives us $L^2 = Y^2 + Y^2 = 2Y^2$. Substituting L=100, we get Y = 100 / (square root of 2) = 100/1.414.

Basically, the Turtle needs to jump horizontally left by (`length/2 + length/1.414`) and vertically down by `length/2`. Using this information, we can create a custom block to draw the octagon.

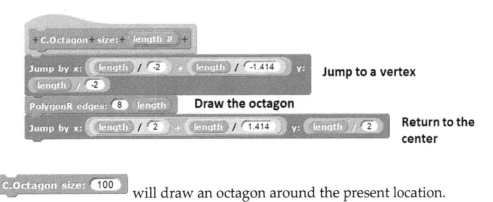

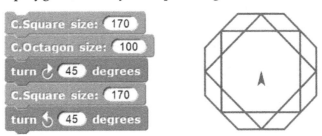 will draw an octagon around the present location.

Designs around a point

Using these new polygons, let's try a simple design.

Programming practice

9. Create the following design using polygons drawn around a center point. <u>Hint</u>: You will need to teach the Turtle how to draw these 3 shapes around a point: (1) circle, (2) point star, and (3) super-octagon.

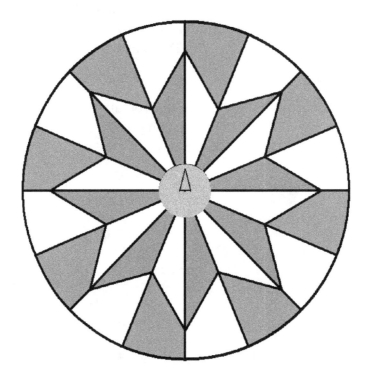

10. Draw the design shown in Figure 8.1. <u>Hint</u>: It uses only two shapes: octagon and square.

Review questions

1. We can create interesting designs on top of ordinary polygons by having the Turtle play a little mischief before drawing every edge of the polygon. For this idea to work, this so-called mischief must:
   a. Turn the Turtle 360 degrees.
   b. Bring the Turtle back to its original position and orientation.
   c. Move less than the length of the edge of the polygon.
   d. Must keep the pen up during the mischief.

2. The following script draws a regular pentagon.

```
repeat 5
  pen down
  move 100 steps
  pen up
  turn ↻ 72 degrees
```

We wish to grow a short whisker at each vertex of this pentagon by inserting the following "mischief".

```
move 50 steps
move -50 steps
```

The modified script is as shown below. It does not draw the whisker as expected but only draws the pentagon as before. What is wrong?

```
repeat 5
  move 50 steps
  move -50 steps
  pen down
  move 100 steps
  pen up
  turn ↻ 72 degrees
```

    a. The pen is not down while drawing the whisker.
    b. The whisker code is placed incorrectly inside the repeat loop.
    c. The whisker code needs to include the command "turn 72 degrees".
    d. You cannot give negative input to the move command.

3. In a so-called "super-polygon" the Turtle draws a full regular polygon on top of each edge of the main regular polygon. For this to work:
    a. Both polygons must have the same number of edges.
    b. The outside polygon must be drawn at 90 degrees to the edge of the inside polygon.
    c. The two polygons must use different colors to be visible.

d. The edges of both these polygons must be of the same length.

4. Inspect the following design and select the correct option.

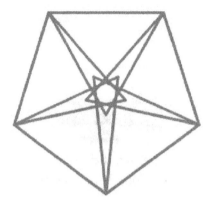

a. This is a super-polygon design in which two triangles are drawn inside each edge of a pentagon.
b. A 5 point star is drawn at the center of a pentagon.
c. This is a super-polygon design in which a triangle is drawn inside each edge of a pentagon.
d. It is not a super-polygon design.

Insights and tips

- Ability to detect basic patterns helps.
- Divide and conquer approach simplifies solutions.
- Generic custom blocks with parameters allow reuse of the same code.
- Code reuse is a must for faster solution development.
- Experimenting with many combinations of parameter values is essential to discover interesting patterns. This also helps in identifying bugs in your code.
- The same design can be created using multiple approaches.
- Knowledge of geometry helps in understanding problems and designing the solutions.

Chapter 9:
Perspectives and Concentric Shapes

My idea of Heaven is to wake up, have a good breakfast, and spend the rest of the day drawing. – Peter Falk

What we will learn in this chapter
- How to create a counter for the REPEAT command using an indexing variable.
- Application of "counters" to draw repetitive patterns in which there is a uniform variation of some kind.
- How to create perspective drawings.

Introduction
Do you like the design shown below?

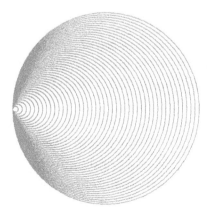

Can you guess how it can be drawn using Turtle commands?

Yes! You can give a series of `circle` commands and increase the size slightly every time. But, that would be tedious, won't it?

How about drawing this beautiful design shown next?

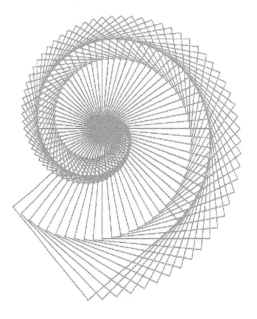

Can you guess how we can draw this design?

If you look carefully, you will see a series of squares drawn around a point, with each square slightly bigger than the previous one. Once again, you could give a series of `square` commands and increase the size slightly every time. But, that would be horribly tedious, wouldn't it!

Continue reading this chapter, if you would like to learn a much more elegant and simpler way of drawing this sort of designs in which there is repetition for sure, but there is a twist after each repetition.

Counting repetitions

Imagine that you want to run around a tree, and your friend is watching you standing aside. You could ask him to count 1, 2, 3... as you go around the tree. So, you could ask him any time, "Hey, what round am I doing now?" And he would tell you, "It's the 9th round", or something like that. In a sense, your friend is your *counter*.

It so happens that we can insert a counter variable inside the Snap REPEAT command and keep track of the number of repetitions.

Counter for the REPEAT Command:

There is no direct way which gives the value of the counter inside REPEAT. Instead, we must insert such a counter ourselves. This can be done using a variable.

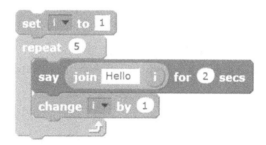

This would make the sprite say "Hello 1", "Hello 2", and so on.

Let's try another example.

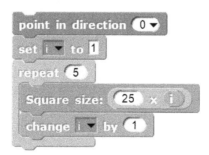

In this case, instead of printing the value of the *counter* we are using it to modify the input of the Square command. See what we get:

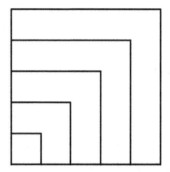

These are 5 squares of sizes 25, 50, 75, 100, and 125 respectively.

Here is the explanation: REPEAT ran the Square command 5 times, but each time the input to Square kept changing - first it was 25*1, second time it was 25*2, and so on. That is why we got 5 squares of increasing size.

Programming practice

1. What will the following instructions do? (Note: You will need to define the triangle procedure first, which will have a size input.)

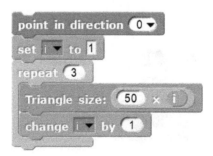

Concentric squares

Now that we have access to the counter of repetitive programs, we will see some interesting applications of this idea of counters.

We will modify the above program of drawing squares to get the design shown below. We will use the  procedure we defined earlier, which draws the square around a center point.

Let's first only draw 4 squares of size 15, 25, 35, and 45:

Since, each square is bigger than the previous one by **10** the above sequence can be re-written as:

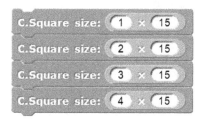

Using a counter variable, we can convert this to a REPEAT instruction as follows:

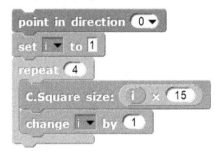

Finally, we can write a procedure to get as *many* squares as we want, with as much *gap* as we want.

```
Inputs:
    Start is the size of the smallest square,
    Step is difference in size between two
        successive squares,
    N is the number of squares.
```

ConcentricSquares start: start # gap: step # count: n #
set i to 0
repeat n
    C.Square size: start + i × step
    change i by 1

See a couple of sample designs below:

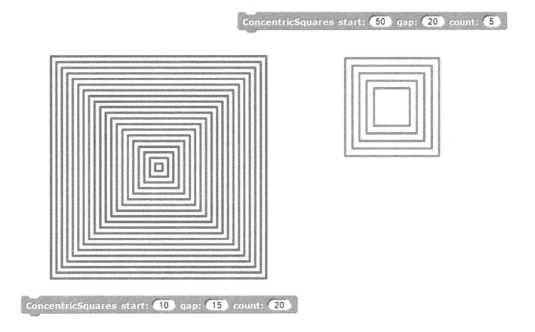

Programming practice

2. You are now ready to try the cone design shown at the beginning of this chapter. (<u>Hint</u>: It is just a series of circles increasing in size.)

3. Try the shell-like design shown after the "cone" design. (<u>Hint</u>: It consists of a bunch of squares gradually increasing in size, with each square drawn at a slight angular offset from the previous one.)

4. Try the following designs.

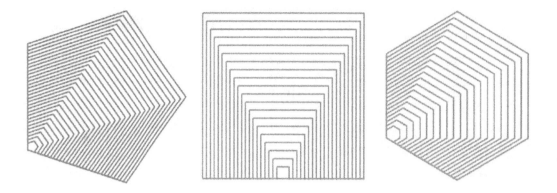

5. Using the ideas we have learnt so far, try the following telescopic arrangement of squares:

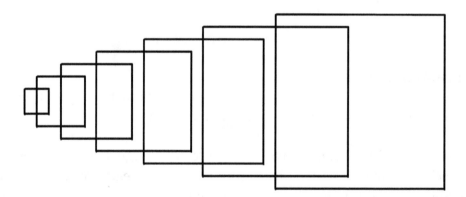

Spirals

As you know, spirals are like tornadoes or whirlpools in which things seem to be getting sucked inside towards the center. See below:

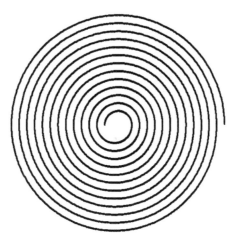

Can you figure out how to draw the above spiral?

Ok, before we tackle this curvy spiral, we will consider a simpler type of spiral - one consisting of straight lines:

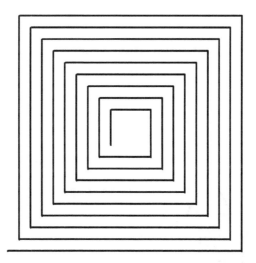

Can you figure out how to draw this one? It's quite straightforward if you look keenly. It's a repetition of move and turn with move's input increasing every time. Using REPEAT and a counter:

```
pen down
set i to 1
repeat 40
    move 5 + 5 * i steps
    turn ↻ 90 degrees
    change i by 1
```

Programming practice

6. Draw the circular spiral shown earlier. (<u>Hint</u>: Consider using part of a circle repetitively).

Perspective drawing

Perspective is nothing but drawing things the way they appear to our eyes. For instance, if we were to look at a row of houses lined one after the other, would they appear like this?

Or, would they appear like this?

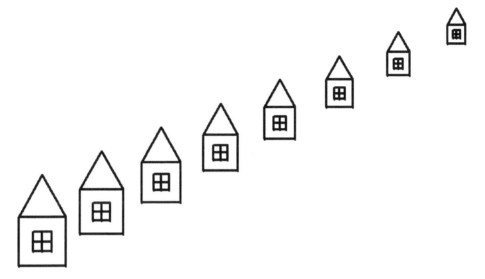

Things in real life appear smaller as they grow distant. This kind of view is called a *perspective view*. Using the idea of counters, we can make our nature drawings look like perspectives!

The idea is simple, really. We have defined earlier, a procedure called MyHouse that takes a scale input for its size (m for size multiplier), which we can use here. The following script would draw the row of equal-size houses shown above. (We will also use the procedure Jump that we designed and used in earlier chapters.)

```
go to x: -230  y: -170
repeat 8
    MyHouse scale: 0.45
    Jump by x: 60  y: 35
```

Now, in order to get a perspective, we just have to make each house appear slightly smaller than the previous one. The following instructions do that job!

```
go to x: -230  y: -170
set i ▼ to 10
repeat 8
    MyHouse scale: 0.45 × 0.1 × i
    Jump by x: 60  y: 35
    change i ▼ by -1
```

Here is a bit of explanation: the biggest house is to be at scale factor 0.45 (as used in the previous example). To make the subsequent houses appear smaller, we will reduce this scale factor – by taking a smaller and smaller fraction. 0.45x1 gives the largest house, 0.45x0.9 gives the next one, 0.45x0.8 the next one, and so on. To get this series 1, 0.9, 0.8, etc. we use the counter variable – but in a decreasing order.

Programming practice

7. Use the trick described above to draw a perspective view of a garden. You can also use it to draw a perspective of a gathering of people.

8. Write a procedure called `Pyramid` that draws a pyramid of equilateral triangles. The procedure takes 2 inputs: the first input specifies the number of triangles at the base of the pyramid, and the second input specifies the size of each triangle. See some example pyramids below:

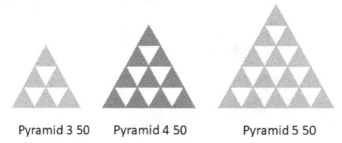

Pyramid 3 50   Pyramid 4 50   Pyramid 5 50

Hint: Use the procedure `ftriangle` to draw a filled triangle. Using `ftriangle`, write a procedure that draws a row of triangles. Finally, with the help of counters in REPEAT, write the `Pyramid` procedure.

9. Write a program to draw the following design. You will need to use the Petal procedure we defined in an earlier chapter.

Review questions:

1. What is wrong with the counter in the following script?

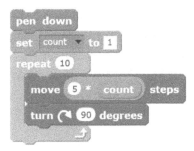

    a. The counter variable must always be named "i".
    b. The counter variable must be used as input to repeat.
    c. The repeat count is too small.
    d. The counter variable is not incremented inside the loop.

2. If the Triangle procedure draws a triangle, what will the following counter script draw?

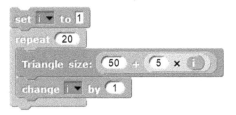

    a. 20 triangles of size ranging from 50 to 100.
    b. 20 triangles of size ranging from 55 to 150.
    c. 20 triangles of size ranging from 1 to 20.
    d. No triangles will be drawn.

Insights and tips

- The counters of REPEAT simply give us a sequence of numbers 1, 2, 3, 4, and so on. Figuring out how to map this sequence to an altogether different sequence of numbers is the *key step* in using these counters to draw innovative designs.

- A simple way to do this is to write in two columns the numbers given by the counter and the numbers that we need. Then, we just have to stare at these two columns long enough to detect the relationship (mathematical connection) between them! Once we detect that connection, it's a matter of converting that *equation* into a Snap program.

Chapter 10:
Fooled by RANDOM

You get pseudo-order when you seek order; you only get a measure of order and control when you embrace randomness. – Nassim Nicholas Taleb

What we will learn in this chapter
- The RANDOM operator.
- Creative use of unpredictability (the RANDOM operator).
- Mapping random numbers to specific characteristics of our designs.

Introduction
One of the most exciting ideas in programming, as in real life, is the idea of *randomness*. We often say things like, "Oh, that's pure luck!" Philosophers often muse about the randomness of events. The industry of gambling is entirely based on the idea of random outcomes. Take a look at the picture below:

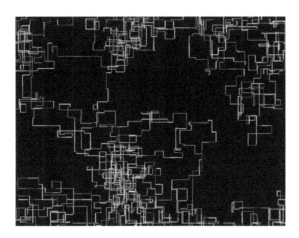

Doesn't it look like a city photographed from space? And would you believe that it is drawn using just a few lines of code?

Read on to understand the magic RANDOM plays in the program above, and to learn how you can creatively use RANDOM in your own programs.

The RANDOM Procedure

Snap offers a simple way to use randomness in programs through the following operator:

This operator returns a number from 1 to 10 – you can't predict what it will return. You can use any range (e.g. -100 to 100); the range can be in any order (e.g. 100 to -100); and it can even be a decimal range (e.g. 1.5 to 11.5).

Let's try a couple of examples.
<u>Note</u>: You must run these instructions a number of times to appreciate their random behavior.

This will print an integer in the range (1 to 100) i.e. less than or equal to 100 and greater than or equal to 1. Every time you run this command you will get a different number in this range!

Programming practice

1. Write a Snap instruction using RANDOM to make the sprite say a number in the range:
    - 500 to 999
    - -200 to 0
    - -0.5 to 9.7

2. The following program draws a wheel of 15 triangles of identical color. Insert the ![set pen color to] command and use RANDOM, such that every triangle is of a different color (as shown).

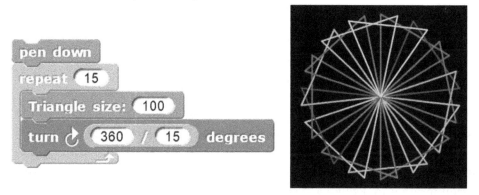

3. Use RANDOM to always get an even number in the range (0 to 200).

RANDOM Designs

Ok, so RANDOM gives us a random number. How do we use that idea? Let us explore and find out. See the design below. We already know how to draw this figure in Snap:

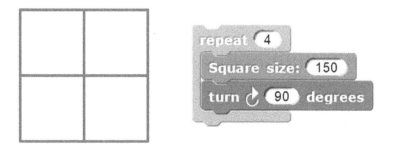

What if we replace the input of Square with a *random* number?

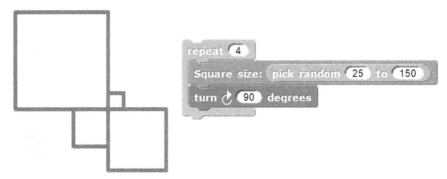

As you can see, we get this weird-looking window. In fact, your window will most likely look quite different! Get it? It's the RANDOM thing!

Now, if we simply put this in a loop and run it a number of times, we get something that looks like a shattered window!

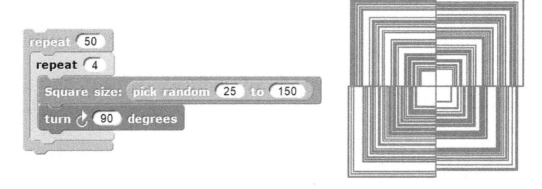

If you increase the outer loop count to a really large number (like 10000) you will just get a large painted square. That's because, when run 10000 times, RANDOM ends up giving practically all possible numbers in the available range (5 to 100), and so, we get squares of all possible sizes drawn very close to each other giving the effect of painting (filling with color).

If called a large number of times, RANDOM usually ends up giving every value in the given range – although it is not predictable when and how often it will give a particular value.

So, as you see, the application of RANDOM really depends on our creativity.

Programming practice

4. See below a peculiar rectangular design that looks vaguely like a city skyline:

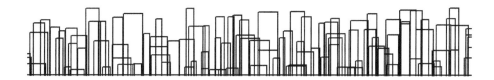

It is actually drawn using the idea of RANDOM. Can you figure out how it is drawn? (<u>Hint</u>: Think about the rectangular wave that we drew some time back).

5. Once you get a working program above, play with it to get very tall buildings, wide buildings, colored buildings, and other interesting variations.

Drawing the space photo

Ok, now that you have a good idea of how RANDOM works, can you figure out how the cityscape (pictured from space) shown at the beginning of this chapter is created? Think about it before reading on.

If you inspect the cityscape closely, you will notice a simple procedure repeated a number times. This procedure consists of the following steps:

-   The Turtle moves some distance forward
-   Then, it either turns left or right, or remains straight

Making step 1 random is easy. But, how about step 2? How can we make the Turtle randomly turn left/right or remain straight? It is as if the Turtle needs to randomly choose from the commands: `turn left 90`, `remain straight`, and `turn right 90`.

Using RANDOM on a set instead of a range:

The above problem can be restated as: Can we use RANDOM to get a number (randomly of course) from the set {-90, 0, 90}? If we can, we will simply provide that number to one of the Turn commands.

This may sound a bit tricky, but it is not all that difficult to work out. Here is how we can do it: There are 3 members in the set, and RANDOM(-1,1) will give us 3 possible outputs in the range (-1 to 1) i.e. -1, 0, and 1. Next, if we multiply by 90, we will get -90, 0, or -90. Get it?

So, the following instruction will give us the required random left/right/straight turn for the Turtle:

(<u>Note</u>: Work out, in your mind, all possible values RANDOM will return above and what the final effect will be.)

With this, can you write the instructions to draw the cityscape?

Using screen space randomly

Here is another interesting use of the RANDOM command. We could draw a number of stars (or any other object really) on the screen as if it were a night sky. We know how to use RANDOM to draw stars of different sizes and even colors. How do we make them appear at *random* locations on the screen?

Think about this a moment before reading on the solution.

Well, it is really quite simple. We could use `go to random position ▼` which would take the sprite to a random place on the screen. Alternatively, we have a procedure called `go to x: ● y: ●` to move our Turtle around the screen. So, all we have to do is *randomize* the inputs of this procedure. Remember that the full size of your visible screen is about 480 steps horizontally and 360 vertically.

The following program draws a starry night sky! The "PointStar" procedure draws a star of N rays each of length L. The script next to it draws the starry sky.

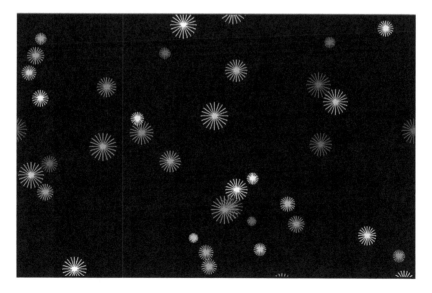

Programming practice

6. Write a program that shows a lot of bubbles floating in air. Each bubble should have a different size (and may be color too) and should appear at a random location on the screen.

7. Draw your other favorite objects at random places on the screen.

Review questions

1. What will the following script draw?

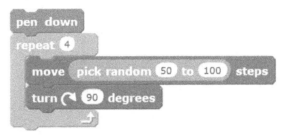

    a. Triangle
    b. Square
    c. 4 parallel lines
    d. Unknown shape

2. To pick a color randomly from red, blue, and green, what range should you use in  ?
    a. 1 to 3
    b. Red to green
    c. 0 to 3
    d. 1 to 10

3. Consider the following instruction:

Which of the following turns is unlikely to result from this instruction?
    a. 0
    b. 45
    c. -45
    d. 60

Chapter 11: Turtles that Climb Trees

To iterate is human, to recurse divine. — L. Peter Deutsch

What we will learn in this chapter

- Recursion: the idea of a procedure calling itself.
- How to use the `wait` command to observe recursion in slow motion.
- The STOP and IF commands to stop recursion.
- How to control recursion using a 'level' input.
- How to design the basic pattern and then draw a tree, with its network of branches, using recursion.

Introduction

Here are some pretty-looking tree drawings including a Fern branch and a Tropical tree:

Believe it or not, these figures have been drawn using Turtle programs – programs containing not more than 15 to 20 instructions each! They are based on an interesting idea called *Recursion*.

Continue reading this chapter to learn about *recursion* and how to draw these sort of designs in Snap.

Mystery of recursion

In order to draw trees like the ones shown above, we will learn about a couple of new blocks ![wait secs] and ![stop all]. But, more importantly, we will explore the interesting and mysterious concept in programming called *Recursive Procedures*.

Definition of Recursive Procedure: A recursive procedure calls itself.

The definition is deviously simple! Let's try it out through an example. Below, see the script for an ordinary custom block in which the Turtle just draws a line and turns right.

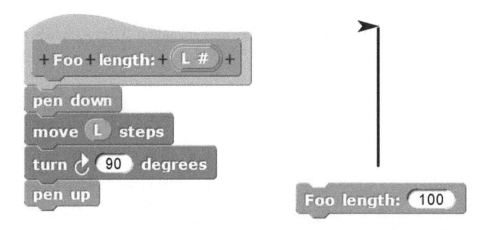

To make this script *recursive*, we will use the custom block *in the script under define block itself*.

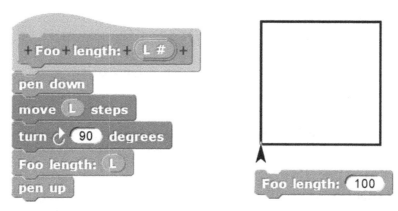

When you run this custom block, you will notice two things: (1) A square is drawn;
(2) It appears as if Snap is hung – our script never stops!

Do you see why our script never stops? If we trace every step in our script we might understand why:

1. First three blocks of Foo draw a line and turn the Turtle to right.
2. Next block calls Foo.
3. First three blocks of Foo draw a line and turn the Turtle to right.
4. Next block calls Foo.
5. First three blocks of Foo draw a line and turn the Turtle to right.
6. Next block calls Foo.
7. …

As you can see, this series of events will never end. After 4 calls a square will be drawn, and after that the Turtle will keep running over that square indefinitely. What we have is a script that will run forever!

(Tip: Click the stop button ⬤ at the top of the screen, to terminate this script.)

Important insight
★ A recursive script can run forever.

Programming practice

1. Create custom blocks for your favorite scripts and make them recursive. See what they do.

Dissecting recursion

Let's now make two small changes (highlighted below) to our recursive script in the custom block Foo and run it again.

With these changes, you will see the Turtle drawing a pattern (a rectangular spiral) as shown below. (It will, in fact, not stop drawing until you terminate the script!)

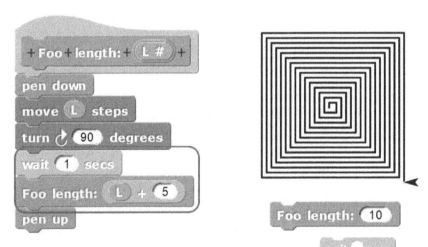

The <u>first change</u> is the insertion of the wait block before the recursive call. Wait causes the program to run in slow-motion, which helps us understand how recursion works. The wait block asks the Turtle to simply do nothing for a specified duration.

The <u>second change</u> affects Foo's input – it is no longer fixed. We start the program with some value (such as 10), and with every subsequent call to Foo, we increase the line length by 5 (from 10 to 15, 15 to 20, 20 to 25, and so on). The wait block allows us to see this process in slow motion.

Programming practice

2. The turning angle in the spiral above is 90. Try changing it slightly (say to 91 or 89) and see what you get. Also try other angles, say 60 or 120. You might get the patterns shown below:

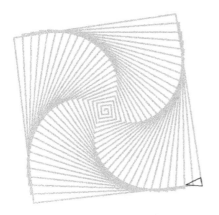 

3. Write a recursive procedure to draw the pattern shown below. (Hint: Start with the biggest square, and in each recursive call, reduce the size of the square in a geometric fashion. For example, each square could be 90% of the previous one.)

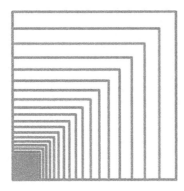

To infinity and beyond!

Writing a script that never terminates is interesting but not very convenient. We would like to write recursive scripts that do interesting things and terminate (i.e. stop) when their job is done.

For this purpose, we will learn about two new command blocks. The first one is called `stop this block ▼` which should only be used inside a custom block: It stops running that custom block.

The STOP block actually has several other variations: `stop all ▼` stops all scripts in your program. This is the same as clicking the stop button at the top of the screen. `stop this script ▼` stops only the current script in which this stop block appears. `stop other scripts in sprite ▼` stops all other scripts for this sprite.

The other command block we will learn about is called `if`. We will first see an example, and then study how `if` works.

<u>Example</u>: The following custom block will draw a square only if its input is greater than or equal to 100.

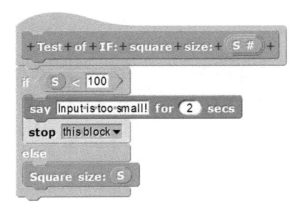

The `if-then-else` block works as follows. If the specified `condition` is true, it runs the blocks inside the `if` portion; if not, it runs the blocks inside the `else` portion.

A *condition* is like a question that can only have two possible answers: **True** or **False**. In the example above, the *condition* is: "Is size less than 100?" If the answer is Yes, or, in other words, if the condition is **True**, the say block will run and then the custom block will stop. If the answer is No, or, in other words, if the condition is **False**, the Square custom block will run.

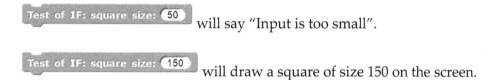 will say "Input is too small".

`Test of IF: square size: 150` will draw a square of size 150 on the screen.

Important insight
- ★ The YES/No question in an if block allows us to conditionally run a set of blocks. That is why we call the question itself a *condition*.

What are the conditions?
Well, the if block and the idea of *conditional execution* are such powerful beasts that we could probably write entire chapters about them. But, for the purpose of using recursion and drawing trees, we need to know just a few more things about conditions.

A comparison between two values is a condition. So, you can use any of the comparison operators like ☐=☐, ☐<☐ or ☐>☐ in your conditions. And we can use ☐ and ☐, ☐ or ☐, and not ☐ logical operators to combine conditions.

Back to recursion

In our `Foo` custom block, we could insert the `if` block to stop the script after a few iterations.

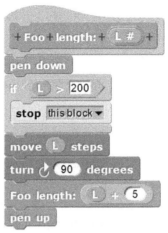

Here, `if` examines the condition: "Is 'L' greater than 200?" If the answer is TRUE, it runs the `stop` command. If the answer is FALSE, it continues with `move`.

If you now run , it will stop when 'L' becomes greater than 200.

Controlling the depth of recursion using "level"

There is another way to make recursion finite – that is, make it stop after some time. We can simply decide how *deep* the recursion should go. See the modified `Foo2` custom block definition below:

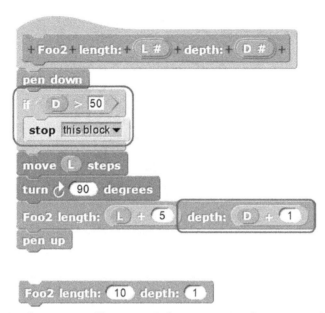

Here, depth is 1 when we call Foo2. It becomes 2 when Foo2 is called the 2nd time. It becomes 3 when Foo2 is called the 3rd time, and so on. IF will cause this recursive chain to terminate when depth becomes 51.

Similar to before, the recursive call increases the length, and it also increases the value of depth by 1. Instead of checking the length, we check depth – which is an indication of how deep the recursion is – and when it reaches 50, we ask the program to stop recursing any further.

Programming practice

4. Modify your earlier recursive scripts such that they do not run forever. Use the IF block to make them stop after doing some work.

5. Earlier we drew a rectangular spiral. Can you draw a real spiral, i.e. a curvy spiral as shown? (Hint: Take the quarter circle custom block you created some time ago and call it recursively with increasing input.) Use the IF block to ensure it stops after some time.

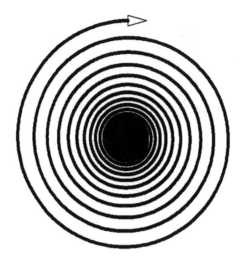

Multiple recursive calls

See a simple recursive design below:

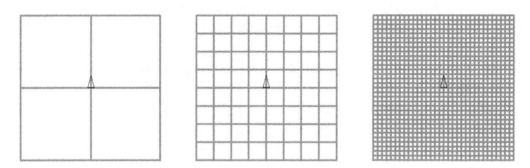

The design itself is quite simple, and can be created using other methods (e.g. by using REPEAT block), but it would be fun to try it using recursion.

The idea is to draw 4 squares in a 2x2 paned-window pattern. Using recursion, we can then go to each square and again draw the 2x2 pattern - one that fits exactly - inside it. This process can go on as *deep* as we wish. The program is shown below.

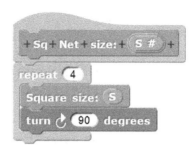

This is our ordinary non-recursive custom block that draws a 2x2 pattern.

Now, the recursive script: Here, we will move the Turtle to the center of each square in the 2x2 pattern and make the recursive call. As before, 'depth' decides when to stop the recursion. Notice that the algorithm makes use of the rotational logic we have used before. At each depth, we start with the square on the top right corner (right of the Turtle as per its orientation), and then go around 4 times, each time turning right by 90 degrees.

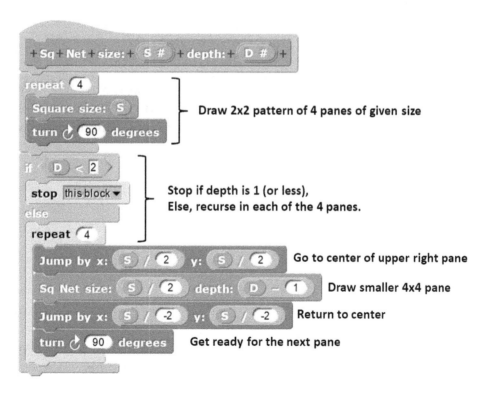

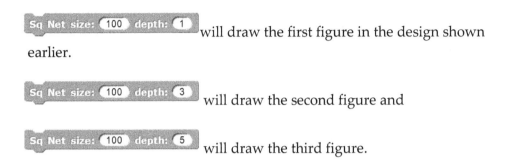 will draw the first figure in the design shown earlier.

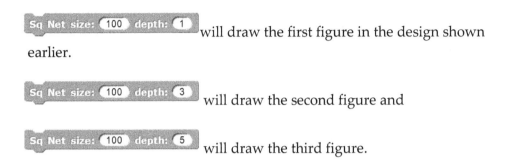 will draw the second figure and

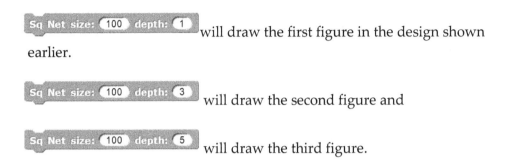 will draw the third figure.

<u>Important</u>: Note above that after each recursive call, the Turtle returns to its original position (as explained in the comments of the program).

Important insight

★ In a recursive program, we can get different designs by controlling the depth of the recursion.

Programming practice

6. The figure below shows a recursive design. It's called "Sierpinski Triangle" named after the Polish mathematician Waclaw Sierpinski. Using the concept of 'level' (depth of recursion), we have shown how this triangle would appear at 3 different levels. Can you work out the script?

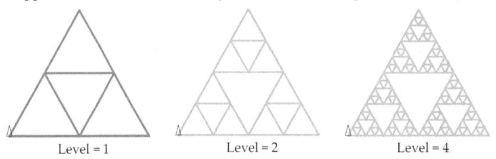

Level = 1   Level = 2   Level = 4

7. Here is another interesting use of recursion – snowflakes! Observe the various levels carefully and work out the recursive procedure.

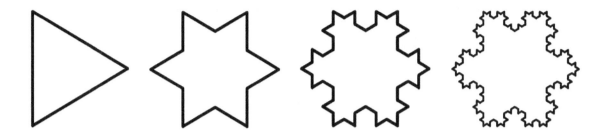

Recursive trees

Ok, after all this hard work and learning, we now have the required arsenal to take on the challenge of using recursion to draw trees.

A tree, as you know, is basically a network of branches. We will see if we can take a simple branch structure and use recursion to grow a tree.

See the Y branch below:

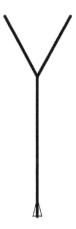

This 'basic tree' can be drawn using the following procedure:

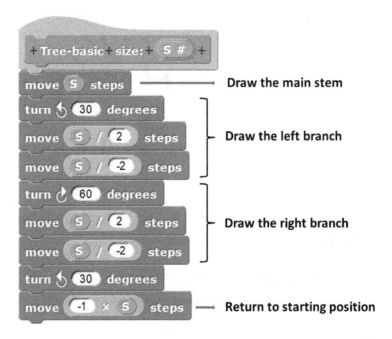

The <u>very important</u> part to remember about drawing such basic patterns for recursive trees is to *always* return the Turtle to the base (original position) and not leave it dangling on the tree somewhere!

Now, using recursion, we will attach similar patterns at the end of each branch of the Y. We will reduce 'size' for the recursive call. To avoid an infinitely running program, we will add a stop condition based on 'level'. That way, we can control how complex the tree should be drawn.

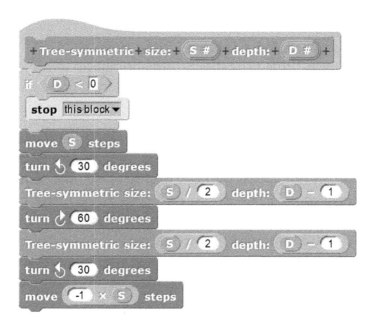

Let's now play with this program and try different values of 'depth'. The following figure shows trees with depth = 1, 3, and 5 respectively.

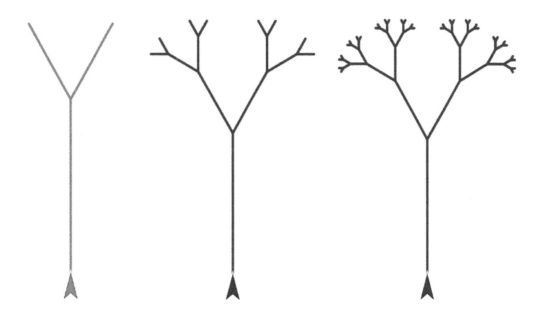

Important insight

★ To write a proper recursive tree procedure, you must
  - ○ Return the Turtle to its starting position, and
  - ○ Insert recursive calls at places where you want branches to grow (usually at end-points).

Programming practice

8. We used certain proportion for each branch in the tree above, and also a certain amount of reduction in size each time the recursive call was made. These parameters obviously determine the appearance of the tree. Modify these values and see what sort of trees you get.

It's a forest out there!

At this point, we are done with learning how to use recursion to draw trees. If you have completely understood how recursive calls help the Turtle climb trees – in a manner of speaking – you are now well on your way to becoming a certified *tree artist*. All you need to do is *experiment with the technique*.

For example, the tree above looks very symmetric. Real trees (with some exceptions, of course) are actually quite asymmetric. How will you draw an asymmetric tree?

The answer is in simply redesigning our basic pattern. See below an example of a quite different basic pattern (containing a main stem and 4 branches), and the basic script do draw that pattern. Note that we have broken up the script simply to show how different parts of the script relate to the parts of the basic pattern. "S" indicates the length of the main stem.

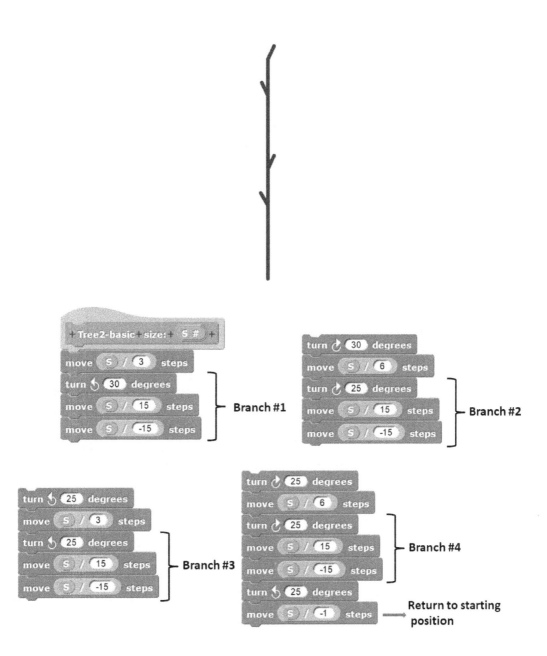

Granted that the basic pattern looks rather ugly; but wait till we apply recursion on it. We will insert 4 recursive calls – one each at the 4 endpoints (of the 4 branches). We will reduce 'size' in each recursive call. The stop condition is based on the concept of 'depth'. Here is the recursive tree procedure. It is once again broken up to show the different parts that relate to the 4 branches.

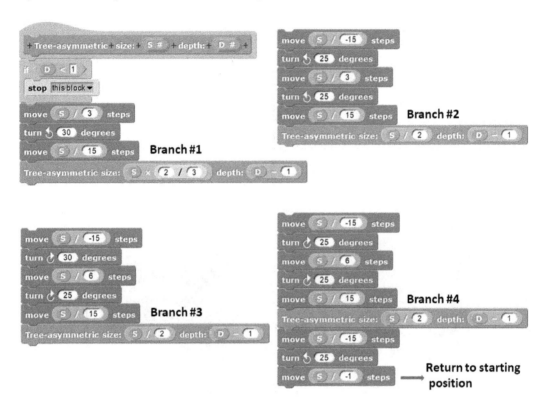

Let's now play with this program for depth = 1, 3, and 6.

Programming practice

9. You can make the tree above more realistic by making the thickness of the branches decrease as you go deeper in the recursion. You can achieve this effect by supplying an additional input for pen size, which should be reduced before it is passed on to the recursive call. With this idea, you can get a tree which would look as shown. Create a custom block for this tree.

10. Create a custom block with a recursive script to draw a symmetric tree (a sort of Christmas tree) as shown here. Use all the ideas we have learnt so far, including the idea of decreasing branch thickness.

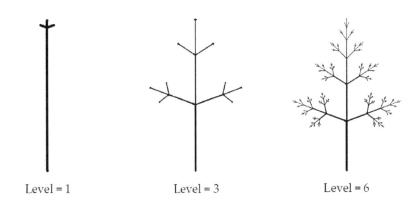

Level = 1   Level = 3   Level = 6

11. You can make the asymmetric tropical tree above even more interesting if you use `pick random ◯ to ◯` in choosing the size of its branches. Experiment with this idea.

12. Try the Fern plant custom block with a recursive script. The following figure shows the result of running this block with 3 different levels.

Level = 2   Level = 3   Level = 4

Hint: The following instructions will draw a single curved line and return the Turtle to its base (this code would actually be level 1 of the recursion):

```
pen down
repeat 10
  move 25 steps
  turn ↻ 5 degrees
repeat 10
  turn ↺ 5 degrees
  move -25 steps
```

You just have to recursively implant the same curved line at a number of places on both sides.

13. The trees shown next have the following new features:

  ○ The tree looks different every time you call the instruction (even if all inputs are the same)
  ○ The tree shows fruit at some places. The fruit shows up at random places, and the amount of fruit is controlled through an input.

• Hints: (1) Obviously, we have used pick random ⬤ to ⬤ block to make things happen differently every time. (2) To draw the fruit, add blocks just before the stop block, because that's where the branches end.

Review questions

1. Recursion is an idea in which:
   a. A script is repeated forever.
   b. A script draws the same design, but smaller and smaller.
   c. A script contains a call to itself.
   d. A script in which the Turtle always comes back to the same place.

2. It is necessary to use the STOP command in recursive scripts because:
   a. Recursion takes the Turtle out of the screen.
   b. Without it the recursion goes on forever.
   c. STOP command brings the Turtle back to its original position.
   d. Recursion slows down all other scripts in your program.

3. The main challenge in drawing recursive designs in Snap is:
   a. Figuring out the basic pattern that will be repeated.
   b. Deciding where to stop the recursion.
   c. Controlling the depth of the recursion.
   d. Getting the Turtle back to its original position.

4. For a recursive script for trees to work properly:
   a. The script must make only one recursive call.
   b. The script must bring the Turtle back to its original state.
   c. The script must use the simplest possible basic pattern.
   d. The script must use a symmetric basic pattern.

Insights and tips

- Recursion is a deceptively simple and tricky idea.
- Sometimes you have to use the stop button at the top of the screen to stop an infinite loop.
- At least one parameter of your recursive procedure must change in a recursive call to make recursion meaningful and useful.
- The condition checked in the IF block must be achievable; otherwise the program will never stop.
- A common bug in recursive programs is not moving the Turtle back to its original position after the recursive call.

Chapter 12: Special Topics

Most good programmers do programming not because they expect to get paid or get adulation by the public, but because it is fun to program. — Linus Torvalds

What we will learn in this chapter
- How multiple Turtles can create exciting new possibilities for Pen Art.
- Turtle Geometry is primarily about relative motion, but, we can also use absolute motion (and thus the XY geometry) to create other interesting designs.

Introduction
Logo, the predecessor of Snap, from where the Pen capability of Snap was inherited, only had a single Turtle sprite. Snap, on the other hand, allows you to have as many "Turtle" sprites as you want. That creates some interesting possibilities, which we will explore in this chapter.

Secondly, the field of Turtle Geometry focuses strictly on the "relative motion" of the Turtle. That is, commands that use the x and y coordinates are rarely used. As a result, most of the work we have explored in the preceding chapters focuses on relative motion of the Turtle. In this chapter, we will explore projects that use the "absolute motion" commands.

We will first briefly explore these concepts and understand how they can be used through concrete examples.

Multiple turtles
Simply stated, in Snap we have multiple Turtles at our disposal that can draw "simultaneously".

For instance, let's say we have two Turtle sprites, and we write the following scripts for them:

For Turtle 1:

For Turtle 2:

If you inspect these scripts carefully, they are almost identical except for the starting location. What will you see if you click the Green flag?

You will see two separate but identical squares drawn at the same time!

One can imagine many exciting applications of this idea. We will use it in the examples discussed later in this chapter.

Absolute motion

Absolute motion refers to motion whose result *does not* depend on your current position and direction. For example, "Going to Washington DC" is absolute motion because you will end up in Washington DC no matter where you currently are.

The following Snap commands (among others) describe absolute motion because the resulting position or direction *does not* depend on the sprite's previous position or direction.

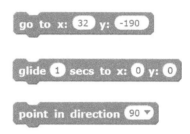

As mentioned above, Turtle Geometry focuses almost entirely on "relative motion", that is, motion in which X and Y coordinates are rarely used.

In the examples below, we will explore how even absolute motion can be used to create some interesting Pen Art.

Kaleidoscope

The kaleidoscope is a tube-shaped optical instrument with two or more reflecting surfaces tilted to each other in an angle, so that one or more (parts of) objects on one end of the mirrors are seen as a regular symmetrical pattern when viewed from the other end, due to repeated reflection.

Our kaleidoscope program will show designs consisting of 4-way symmetry, i.e. each design will be duplicated 4 times. To do this, we will need 4 sprites. Each sprite will draw with a different pen color. Each sprite's movement is based on the movement of the mouse. The first sprite follows the mouse. The other 3 sprites move around as the mouse moves, but reflected over the X and Y axes.

See the design below drawn by such a kaleidoscope program.

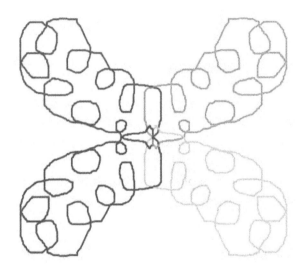

High level design:

Let's take a look at the main screen of the program and try to point out the different features. Below we show a sample design again with the XY stage. We have named the quadrants Alpha, Beta, Gamma, and Delta.

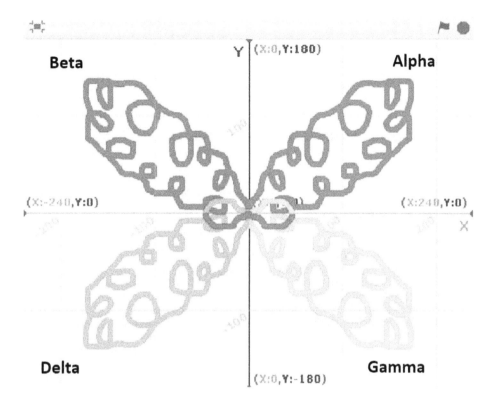

We can allocate each Turtle sprite one of these quadrants. The main sprite will draw in one of the quadrants, say the Alpha quadrant, and the remaining 3 will mimic its movements but in their respective quadrants.

Initial version:

In the initial version of the program, we will work on the following feature ideas:
- Start with 4 Turtle sprites. Each Turtle will control one quadrant of the Snap screen.
- Teach the main Turtle sprite to draw on the screen by following the mouse pointer. Have special keys to set the pen up and down.
- Teach the remaining sprites to imitate the main Turtle's movements by transposing X and Y coordinates. Use the same keys to set their respective pens up and down.

Feature Idea # 1:

Start with 4 Turtle sprites. Each Turtle will control one quadrant of the Snap screen. Teach the main Turtle sprite to draw on the screen by following the mouse pointer. Have special keys to set the pen up and down.

Design:

Load any 4 sprites and use them as they are, or give them a Turtle costume.

The main Turtle sprite can follow the pointer by continuously copying its X and Y coordinates. These are available in the ⬭mouse x⬭ and ⬭mouse y⬭ properties. The following script will do this job:

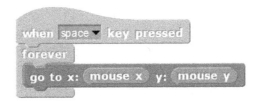

When the pen is down, the Turtle will draw whatever freehand design the user draws by moving the mouse pointer.

Feature Idea # 2:

Teach the remaining sprites to imitate the main Turtle's movements by transposing X and Y coordinates. Use the same keys to set their respective pens up and down.

Design:

This is the main crux of the kaleidoscope design, which is based on the idea of reflection.

We have the main Turtle (let's call it A) drawing in the upper-right "Alpha" quadrant in which both X and Y coordinates are positive. The second Turtle will create a reflection of whatever A draws in the "Beta" quadrant. How can it do that?

To understand how this could be done, let's draw a straight line at 45 degrees in Alpha quadrant, and its reflection in Beta quadrant, as shown below.

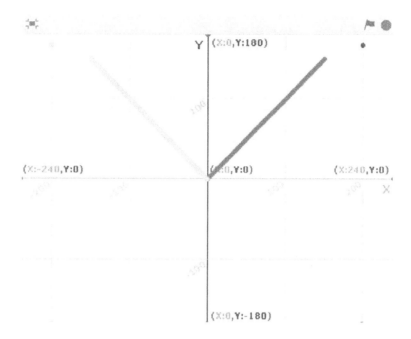

If you observe carefully, you will notice that every point on the reflected line in Beta quadrant has the same value of Y and negative value of X of the corresponding point on the original line in Alpha quadrant.

So, all that the Turtle B has to do is take the negative of mouse x. The following script would do this for Turtle B.

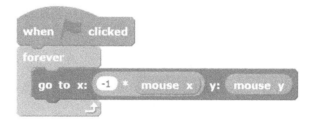

Programming practice

1. Based on what we did for Turtle B, write scripts for Turtle C and D and complete the Kaleidoscope program for freehand designs.

2. What if the main Turtle in the Kaleidoscope drew some specific design instead of freehand drawing? (See below for a sample.) It would no longer help for other Turtles to use X and Y of the mouse pointer. Design an alternate approach for this type of Kaleidoscope design. (Hint: Consider having them follow the main Turtle instead using some of its properties (built-in variables).)

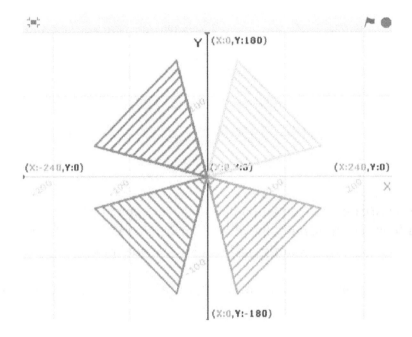

Clones doing Pen Art
When we discussed multiple Turtles above, you might have already thought about using clones to do interesting parallel designs. You are right! The idea of clones creates a whole new universe of possibilities.

Here is a simple example. Some time ago, we drew a night sky of colorful stars as in the figure below. We did this using a single Turtle. Can we do the same thing using clones this time?

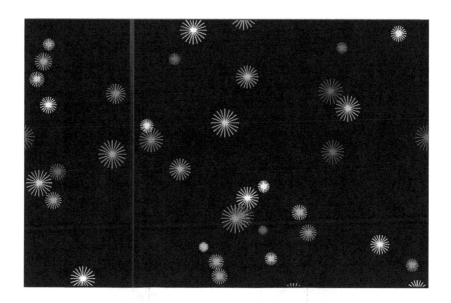

We already know how to draw a single point-star. Let's say we have a custom block called PointStar that can draw a point star of any number of rays and size. We also know how to create clones. Can we then ask each clone go to a random location on the screen and draw a point star?

Yes, the following script demonstrates how this can be done:

```
when I start as a clone
hide
set x to (pick random (-220) to (220))
set y to (pick random (-150) to (150))
set pen color to (pick random (1) to (200))
set N ▾ to (pick random (20) to (80))
set size ▾ to (pick random (10) to (30))
PointStar len: (size) rays: (N)
delete this clone
```

Fabric Design

We will present a program that directly uses Snap's XY screen. See the design below:

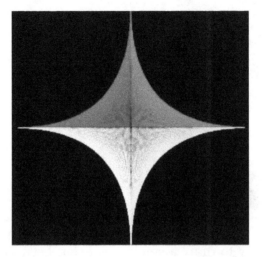

It looks like a complicated design, but, really it just contains a large number of straight lines. If we run the same program but reduce the crowding of lines a bit, see what we get:

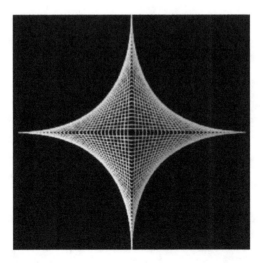

Can you see the straight lines crisscrossing across the X and Y axes?

Let's reduce the crowding even further to understand the idea better:

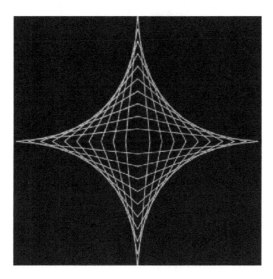

As you can see now, this design connects N equally-spaced points on each side of the X axis with the same number of equally-spaced points on each side of the Y axis. In the figure just above, for example, N = 10.

Each point on the Y axis is connected (by straight lines) with two points on the X axis – one on left and one on right, and vice versa. The connections are asymmetric – that is, the farthest points (from the center) on the X axis are connected to the closest points (from the center) on Y axis – thus creating the impression of a nice curvature (although there is no curved line).

Design:
Let's do one more round of the program with N = 4 and see what we get.

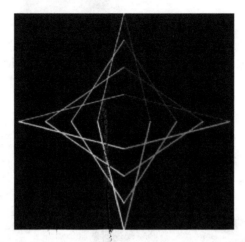

By observing these different outputs of the same program, we can devise the following algorithm:

<u>Input:</u>
N: number of points (as discussed above)
TL: half width/height of the design (should be <= 180 on Snap screen)

<u>Variables:</u>
L (gap between each pair of points) = TL/N
x1, y1, x2, y2 for endpoints of each line to be drawn

<u>Algorithm for the upper half of the design:</u>
We will start from the origin and move *up* on the Y axis. For each point on Y axis we will connect it with two points on the X axis as shown below:

```
Initially: Point1: (x1=0, y1=L); Point2: (x2=TL, y2=0)
Repeat N times:
      Connect point1 and point2
      Reverse sign of x2
      Connect point1 and point2
      Reverse sign of x2
      y1 = y1 + L
      x2 = x2 - L
End-Repeat
```

Algorithm for the lower half of the design:

We will start from the origin and move *down* on the Y axis. For each point on Y axis we will connect it with two points on the X axis as shown below:

```
Initially: Point1: (x1=0, y1=L); Point2: (x2=TL, y2=0)
Repeat N times:
      Connect point1 and point2
      Reverse sign of x2
      Connect point1 and point2
      Reverse sign of x2
      y1 = y1 - L
      x2 = x2 - L
End-Repeat
```

Programming practice

3. Using the algorithms given above write a complete program to draw the Fabric design for any value of N. Assign 4 different random colors to the 4 quadrants of the design.

4. The upper and lower halves of the fabric design are independent of each other and hence can be drawn by two Turtles working in parallel. Modify the above program and divide the work between 2 Turtles.

5. Instead of the asymmetric connections of the Fabric design, create a design in which points on X axis connect with points on Y axis symmetrically. See a sample output below.

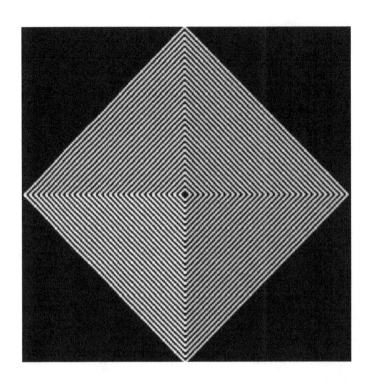

Appendix A: The FILL Library

www.ingramcontent.com/pod-product-compliance
Lightning Source LLC
Chambersburg PA
CBHW080553060326
40689CB00021B/4847